Nov 21, 2002

George,

To be a firefighter is a great honor. Our mission is to save lives. I enjoyed meeting you on the Queen of the West and I hope you enjoy my stories.

Stay safe,

"*Only people can prevent fires. We must become constantly alert to the threat of fires to ourselves, our children, and our homes. Fire is almost always the result of human carelessness. Each one of us must become aware – not for a single time, but for all the year – of what he or she can do to prevent fires.*"

PRESIDENT RICHARD M. NIXON, September 7, 1972
From *America Burning*, The Report of the National Commission on Fire Prevention and Control

Captain, He Bought Eggs

*This book is dedicated to the families of the brother
and sister firefighters who unselfishly went to work one
day and never came home. May the memories of these
heroes allow us to realize how precious life is, and how
their sacrifice has made our careers and lives a little safer
each morning when we wake up.*
Carmine Speranza

*To know even one life has breathed easier because you
have lived...this is to have succeeded.*
Ralph Waldo Emerson

Captain, He Bought Eggs

By Carmine Speranza

STORIES OF A FIREFIGHTER
TOLD TO AND PHOTOGRAPHED
BY BETH REYNOLDS

Carmine Speranza [signature]

THE PHOTO-DOCUMENTARY PRESS, INC.
ST. PETERSBURG, FLORIDA

Printed in the United States of America
Copyright © 2001 The Photo-Documentary Press, inc.

All rights reserved. No part of this publication may be used or reproduced in whole or in part, in any form beyond that allowed by Sections 107 and 108 of the U.S. Copyright Law and except by reviewers for public press without the written permission of

The Photo-Documentary Press, inc.
P. O. Box 10064
St. Petersburg, Florida 33733
photodocumentarypress.com
(727) 896-5656

LCCN: 2001 130777
ISBN: 0-9673284-1-1

Design: Voshardt/Humphey Artworks, St. Petersburg
Editor: Clint Page, St. Petersburg
Printed by: Rose Printing Company, Tallahassee

TABLE OF CONTENTS

FOREWORD

TO BE A FIREFIGHTER has been one of the greatest opportunities for me.

We work at a job that allows us to make a difference in people's lives. To save a human life is our first and greatest mission.

Being a firefighter requires both the physical and mental ability to perform a very demanding job, a job that must be done many times in the face of great danger and done without hesitation.

To be called a good "fireman" is the greatest compliment among firefighters. To attain this status you must start out early in your career and get "into" the job. This means learning all you can about how to do your job. You must practice every skill needed, so you will do well when the time comes. Work hard at every job you do, especially when operating at fires and other emergency operations.

You must master all the procedures and techniques required to do the job and know them well enough to teach others. Then you will be "into the job" and not just on the job.

There are three things that may give status among firefighters.

SENIORITY: Time on the job grants a certain amount of respect and consideration. Seniority has its place. A senior member with great skill and ability will create enormous respect. Seniority without skill is meaningless and embarrassing to the senior member and dangerous to the junior member.

At left:
The original brass pole from 3 Station.

RANK: Rank grants legitimate authority and responsibility for those under your command. Use this power wisely and bring those under you up to the highest level of performance especially at emergency situations. Your skill and ability will be the example that they will follow.

Remember, you can't hide behind your rank.

REPUTATION: Your reputation is the most important thing you have. It takes time to build up the knowledge and skill needed to do the job well and you must be tested under fire conditions and excel at these critical times in order to gain a good reputation as a "fireman."

Remember you can lose a good reputation a lot faster that you can build one up.

Always be accountable for your actions and act responsibility.

Always work with the newest members and make their training a priority.

A new firefighter walks into the department with a blank slate. His reputation, whatever he puts on it, is his and his alone.

What I realized after many years is that this is much more than a job or even a career. It is an opportunity to learn new lessons about yourself.

FIREMAN ROBERT REX MORRIS
STAMFORD FIRE DEPARTMENT, 1970–1973
CURRENTLY, CAPTAIN, LADDER 28 FDNY

Dedicated to my father
Fireman Thomas Anthony Morris, 1911–1978

INTRODUCTION

© Christine Breslin

I ADMIT I KNEW NEXT TO NOTHING ABOUT FIREFIGHTERS or fire science when I started this project. I thought I would have to do an endless amount of research to educate myself. I was wrong. All I had to do was listen – listen to the stories of a man who has dedicated his life to being a firefighter.

I thought Carmine Speranza was a special firefighter. I was wrong again. Over the ten months it took to produce this book I met many firefighters and they were all the same – heroes.

That is an accurate word; you will see it in many of Carmine's stories. Firefighters are men and women who knowingly risk their lives for us. They all speak the same language, and they share a passion that runs so deep that it cannot be changed or erased from their genetic make-up. They did not pick a job. Most firefighters are born to it.

Carmine said he had always wanted to do a book about his career and the politics involved in being a chief officer, but the stories he told about his days on the line were so visually stimulating to me that I knew I had to put his words and my images together. His memories are so clear and fresh in his mind, that he can almost relive each day of his career and smile while doing it. He loved every single minute he was a firefighter.

I believe that my passion for combining words and images runs as deep as Carmine's passion for fighting fires. Like the heroes of this book, I cannot imagine having another career.

I combine photographs and words rather than single images because this process takes me through time and creates a more complete story. Projects may take up to a year creating a bond and a sense of trust between photographer and subject. I have this strong desire not only to take pictures but also to share the experiences of my subjects and hopefully to give something back to them through the act of recording their lives.

I would like to thank Carmine Speranza for his stories, Clint Page for his editing, and Robyn Voshardt and Sven Humphrey for their design, which makes us all look good.

BETH REYNOLDS
SEPTEMBER 2001

THE BRICK

THE ORDINARY BRICK measures two inches by three inches by eight inches and weighs two pounds, which makes it an effective door stop. But the brick that holds open the door to Carmine Speranza's home office is no ordinary brick. For one thing, it has his name carved into it. For another, it has been etched by his life.

When Carmine came to 3 Company in 1971, he found himself at one of Stamford's oldest firehouses. It stood on a hill at the corner of Fairfield Avenue and West Main Street, overlooking most of downtown Stamford. When it was built in 1910, the equipment – pumps and steamers – was drawn by horses. The poured concrete floor was cut by half-inch deep grooves into 12-inch squares to give traction for the horses pulling the heavy fire pumps. The watch desk he would man for hours on end was made of red brick with a charcoal slate top. The plaster walls were a faded moss green, and the paint on the ceiling was peeling. Everything was dark from years of soot, dirt, and smoke. In damp weather you could smell the remnants of past fires fought. And outside were all the places where he carved his name in the brick walls.

It was tradition, he remembers, for firefighters of his generation to carve their names in the bricks of the stations in which they served. "There were very few names carved when I arrived in 1971." In the years he was there, Carmine carved somewhere between twenty-five and fifty bricks.

Carmine was on vacation when the old firehouse was razed in the 1980s. When he got back, he went to retrieve one of the bricks he had carved in his seven years at 3 Company. He could recall where most of them were when the building was standing. "I can remember going to the roof of the building and attempting to hang over and carve my name off the parapet." But as he stood on the hill, looking at the large piles of debris, he knew he had little, if any, chance of finding them now.

In July of 1993, Carmine retired. In 24 years with the Stamford Fire Department, he had risen through the ranks to become the city's chief fire marshal. Speeches were given, people stood and applauded. And then Rick Miller, a dedicated firefighter from 3 Company, came forward to say a word. In his hand was something wrapped in tinfoil. Rick spoke of the brothers who had passed, thanked Carmine for his dedication, and then turned and gave him his tinfoil-wrapped present. "When he handed it to me, I realized it was a brick."

But not just any brick. It was one of those that Carmine had carved over the years. "I never knew he had it," Carmine said. "Rick always was one for preserving tradition." Miller, who had lived near the firehouse, had picked through the remains of the old 3 Company firehouse and saved the carved bricks. "It was a pretty touching moment. I had a great career. It made you think of all the good times you had there."

The building is gone. It exists only in memories, photographs, home movies, and a few cherished bricks. Bricks like Carmine's.

IT WAS TRADITION, HE REMEMBERS, FOR FIREFIGHTERS OF HIS GENERATION
TO CARVE THEIR NAMES IN THE BRICKS OF THE STATIONS IN WHICH THEY SERVED.

First Memory

ALTHOUGH NOT ALL OF THE DETAILS ARE CLEAR, Carmine's first memory of firefighters is sharp in his mind. It must have been cold: the coal furnace was heating the house. He must have been four or five: he was at home, not in school. It was morning: he had not been out to play yet.

Carmine lived with his mother and father on Victory Street in Stamford on the second floor of a frame house; his grandfather, aunt, and uncle lived on the first floor. It was an old house with a coal-fired furnace in the basement. Young Carmine was accustomed to hearing coal sliding down a chute into the basement. What he was not accustomed to was sirens.

What was even more unexpected was that the truck and engine from 3 Company stopped directly in front of the house and driveway. Carmine had a great view of the action as the firemen dealt with a fire in the Speranza's chimney. "My mother put me in a chair, a high back chair, and wrapped me in blankets. I don't mean one blanket or two blankets. I remember she wrapped me, like the Pillsbury Dough Boy." She took him downstairs from the second floor and placed him facing out of one of the six-foot dining room windows on the first floor where he could see the truck and engine and the firefighters. "That was my first experience with seeing the fire department in action."

They had to get to the roof to clear the chimney. "Back in those days the firemen wore rubber rain coats. I remember them putting a wooden ladder up." The ladder was so close he could almost reach out and hold it for them as they went up to knock down the fire in the chimney. They had ropes with chains on the end of them, and when they would swing the ropes inside the chimney, they would clear out the soot, pitch, and creosol that was burning inside it.

There was no damage to the house, and everyone was safe. Carmine's recollection ends there. Well, almost ends there. Ask him about the last thing he remembers of that day, and he says, nodding his head with assurance: "My mother took me outside to look at the fire engines."

THE LADDER WAS SO CLOSE HE COULD ALMOST REACH OUT AND HOLD IT FOR THEM AS THEY WENT UP TO KNOCK DOWN THE FIRE IN THE CHIMNEY.

Upside Down

FROM THE MORNING THEY CAME TO HIS HOUSE to put out a chimney fire, young Carmine idolized the firefighters of 3 Company. For a boy in those days, career choices were simple. A boy wanted to grow up to be a fireman, a policeman, or a baseball player. Carmine made his choice early.

The firehouse was right across the street from Stevens Elementary School, and five days a week he walked past the firehouse where he would eventually work. If the big apparatus doors were open, he would stop at the station. Often he was dismissed and told to "go play." But one afternoon, when he detoured past the firehouse on his way home from school, somebody actually talked to him.

"I met a man on the watch desk one day," Carmine remembers. "He had slippers on, brown, corduroy slip-ons." This was the first time anybody in the firehouse took a minute to speak to him, and what he heard, he could hardly believe. "The only way you can become a fireman is you have to climb the pole upside down," he said. Carmine stood before him perplexed. "I didn't know how you could do that." But he thought, *apparently all the people who worked in this station did this.* He went home and told the story to his father who told him it probably wasn't true. But Carmine couldn't take that risk.

In physical education class at school that week, the boys were learning how to climb ropes. Zipping up to the top of the rope the normal way was no problem for Carmine. "That was a piece of cake. But in my mind I was thinking, somehow I've got to climb this rope upside down, so I could see how hard it is to do."

From the gym, Carmine could see 3 Station across the street. That was all the motivation he needed. In the gymnasium, the ropes hung from the tall ceiling, waiting. After school, when no one else was around, he decided to try. He tried and tried – for fifteen minutes, he tried – to climb the rope upside down. "I couldn't even get upside down and grab the rope. I remember how sad I was that I couldn't even do that." He walked home heavy-hearted.

A few days later he went back to the firehouse. He had to know how they climbed the pole upside down. He wanted someone to show him how to do this so he could go practice. After all, he was going to be a fireman. There was a different man on the watch desk. Carmine asked if you had to climb the pole upside down to be a fireman. "He laughed, and he said, 'No, you *slide down* the pole, you don't *climb up* the pole.'" Carmine said another fireman had told him about climbing up the pole, but he was assured that it was not true. "That was a tremendous relief."

Carmine smiles as if this had happened yesterday. "I believed these guys," he says. "They were my heroes." The boy who would become chief fire marshal of Stamford, Connecticut, had spent two weeks wondering how he would become a fireman if he couldn't meet the challenge tossed at him by his hero in corduroy slippers. "I wish I could have met him after I came on the job so I could tell him how he affected me. And ask him to show me how *he* climbed the pole upside down."

At right:
The Steven's School Gymnasium where Carmine climbed the ropes. It is now the Yerwood Community Center.

Turn of River Fire Department

When Carmine was seven years old, his family moved from the West Side of the city to an area known as Turn of River in the northern part of Stamford.

The area was a residential neighborhood of single family homes, protected by a volunteer fire department, which had a paid driver who would take the lead engine to the fire scene. Carmine still wanted to someday be a fireman. He soon discovered that the Turn of River Fire Department was located eight houses up his street. But his elementary school was in the opposite direction. So for years, he never walked up that way. "Most of my friends lived within a few houses," he says, "and having strict parents I really didn't wander very far."

There was a large air horn on top of the station, and when it blew, he says, "I knew there was a fire and a good chance I would see an engine go by my house." His next door neighbor was a teenage volunteer and he would give Carmine the run-down on any fires he had gone to. Most were grass or leaf fires, nothing catastrophic, Carmine says, "But I remember how important he sounded when he spoke to me."

During Fire Prevention Week, the engine would come to school. "I clearly remember holding the booster line and being allowed to pull the trigger on the nozzle while a fireman knelt down beside me. The recoil sticks in my mind." Today he wonders at what pressure the engine was pumping. After all, how much could a sixth grader handle?

The older he got the more freedom he had, and so began many hours of hanging out at the fire station.

A paid engine driver named Woody Smith took Carmine under his wing, which gave him the opportunity to become familiar with the equipment. "He would use me to check the lights, help fill the booster tank and check and change the oxygen tanks on the resuscitator. Once in a while, he would give me the famous firehouse quote that I had become used to hearing: 'Go play now.'"

By the time he started high school, Carmine knew where every piece of equipment was located on both engines and how to use all of them. The chief at the time was a pipe-smoking house painter named Benny Shute, and the fire marshal was a genius named Tommy Ritchie. "Tommy worked in a bank but knew a tremendous amount about fire." He taught the probationary classes that all members had to pass.

In January of 1964 Carmine was seventeen, the minimum age for becoming a volunteer fireman. He turned in his application, which was posted on the station's bulletin board for thirty days so all members could view it. Three negative votes from the membership would be enough to keep him out. In February, he became a probationary fireman of the Turn of River Volunteer Fire Department. "I practically lived at the firehouse, coming home only to eat and sleep. If my girlfriend wanted to find me, she knew to go to the firehouse." Drills were the second and forth

There was no doubt in my mind that I wanted to be a professional fireman.

Monday nights; meetings were the first and third. "Little did I know this volunteer fire department was pouring the foundation for my future," Carmine says. "There was no doubt in my mind that I wanted to be a professional fireman."

For about eight months, he responded to brush and car fires, running to the station each time the horn blew.

Then he experienced his first working structure fire – a house on Dunn Avenue. When they arrived, there was grayish smoke coming from the two-and-a-half-story wood frame house. It was dark and cold. The captain at the time was Pete Canzano, and says Carmine, "He told me, 'Grab an inch-and-half and let's get in there.'"

They entered through the front door and crawled to the rear of the house where the kitchen was located. "Fire was coming out of the cellar door and dancing on the ceiling," Carmine remembers. To a teenage volunteer working his first house fire, the sounds and the sight of fire coming out of the basement door were unbelievable. The wood and paint were crackling and popping, the glass windows breaking.

"I had the nozzle, and Pete was right behind me. I knew Pete had years of shipboard fire fighting experience having been in the Coast Guard." Carmine felt safe with Pete behind him telling him what to do with the nozzle. "I remember Pete felt the pressure was too high on the handline. He yelled back to someone outside to cut the pressure down. In seconds our line went limp. No water, just drops. Pete yelled 'Back out, back

out.'" He ripped into the pump operator who misunderstood and shut their line down. The problem solved, Pete said, "Let's get back in there."

By that time the fire was in the front room. "I remember just opening the nozzle and swirling it around the ceiling," says Carmine, but he doesn't recall much else about his first structure fire.

Back at the station, they had to wash the hose and put dry hose back on the engine. All equipment had to be wiped down and back in its place. Everyone had a story about what they did at the scene.

The women's auxiliary brought them coffee and donuts during the cleanup. The food quickly disappeared. "It was after midnight when I walked home. I don't know if my feet ever touched the ground." As he lay in bed he relived the night's events over and over. "I had just gone to my first structure fire and could not wait to tell my parents and friends."

Hundreds of volunteers have passed through the Turn of River Volunteer Fire Department. Benny and Tommy have passed on, but Pete Canzano, 86 years old, can still be found at the fire station on Monday nights, teaching new volunteers about fire. Maybe one day one of those young men – or women, now – will say, as Carmine does, "The Turn of River Volunteer fire Department allowed me to get hands-on experiences in the profession that I had dreamed about."

Taking the Test

When he was discharged from the Army in 1968 (he was drafted in 1966), Carmine was twenty-one and ready to take the fire department test. Stamford gave the test approximately every two years, so Carmine had to wait almost a year for his chance to take his test. "Although I don't remember the date or place of the test I do know I received a letter from the City of Stamford dated January 17, 1969 stating I had passed."

Then came a physical exam, which produced another form, this one signed by a city physician, stating; "I have found him qualified physically for the duties of fireman." Finally, five years after Carmine joined the Turn of River Volunteer Fire Department, it was beginning to look as if a professional fire fighting career was in his grasp.

His parents, with whom he lived, made it very clear that he was not going to sit home and wait for the job. They strongly suggested he not quit the job he held in an electronics company that made ticker tape machines for the stock market. After all, the company had held his position when he was drafted. "My mother felt the future was electronics, and she was very wise to make that prediction but I wanted my future to be the Fire Department."

In June 1969, the city notified Carmine that he was to be hired as a fireman. "Unfortunately, the call came when I was at work and my mother took the message. I had to wait until the next day to return the call during my morning break."

The Lieutenant said Carmine could come downtown, sign his papers, and pick up his gear. He instantly faked an illness, a neat trick with a big smile on his face. "I'm sure I did not convince him [his boss] but he did let me go with only a question or two." Excited and very nervous, he wasted no time driving downtown. He parked behind Fire Headquarters and entered through the open green back door that led to the apparatus floor. "This was my first time ever in this building. In my mind, the ceilings looked about fifty feet high and the apparatus floor looked huge. One bay was empty, only the drip pan sat shining on the floor." He proceeded to the watch desk. "I remember saying, 'I'm going to be a new fireman, how do I get to the second floor to sign the papers?'" The fireman congratulated Carmine, shook his hand, and showed him the stairs that took him to the second floor administration area.

Upstairs he met two other new hires, Jerry and Pete, who were also there to sign their papers. When they were done, the new firemen were taken to a clothing storage area that smelled, Carmine remembers, like new rubber.

They started trying on equipment. "What a feeling! It was like someone had given me a million dollars. My own, my very own gear was somewhere in this room." Helmets were lined up on a shelf in all different sizes. "My head was in the clouds. After trying a few helmets on I picked the Cairns helmet that fit me perfectly." It was shiny black leather, not equipped with the flip-down eye protection that later became common. His brand new black rubber coat had S F D stenciled on the back in eight-inch letters. Boots were lined up against the walls. He tried on several pairs. "Finally, I choose the boots that would complete my protective equipment."

"I held my boots in my left hand, with my coat tucked under the same arm, and I wore my helmet. I was ecstatic. Nothing could be better." A man stopped the three of them in the hall and said the chief of the department wanted to meet them. "I remember shaking hands with about five people. I have no idea who they were, but they were in the office and must have been important." One said to Jerry, "You gonna drive home with your boots on?" and then turned to Carmine and asked, "You gonna sleep with that helmet on?"

The new firefighters were given their assignments. Carmine was to go into group #4 under the direction of Deputy Chief John Boesen. Group #4 was starting nights. "My first night was July 4, 1969. Working a forty-two-hour week, my starting pay would be $7,525 per year." No wonder most firefighters had second jobs.

"When I went home that afternoon I placed my boots in the living room under one of the windows, my coat folded neatly in front and my helmet, which I did take off to drive home, on top of the coat." A shrine had been created in the Speranza house.

The next day Carmine went to work and gave his two-week notice. During his exit interview someone from personnel told him, "You'll make a lot more money staying here and you'll have every weekend off." Carmine thought to himself, *Thanks but no thanks, I'm outta here.*

MY FIRST NIGHT WAS JULY 4, 1969. WORKING A FORTY-TWO-HOUR WEEK, MY STARTING PAY WOULD BE $7,525 PER YEAR. NO WONDER MOST FIREFIGHTERS HAD SECOND JOBS.

EVEN THOUGH HE WAS THE JUNIOR MAN, HE HAD A ROOM OF HIS OWN, A LUCKY BEGINNING.

First Night

One evening in July 1969, Carmine showed up for his very first shift as a professional firefighter. *This is it*, he thought. *My dream has come true*. He was finally a member of Local 786, International Association of Firefighters. He was assigned to Headquarters, also known as 1 Company; he was on nights, 6:00 p.m. to 8:00 a.m., for the first rotation. "I was twenty-two. I had a smile from ear to ear," he says. But he was nervous and apprehensive, wondering if he would measure up to the more experienced firefighters. He arrived more than thirty minutes early.

Carmine had been a volunteer firefighter since he was seventeen years old. But this was different. *I am finally getting to be a firefighter and they're going to pay me for it*. He was the only new guy on this shift and he soon realized he was the youngest man working in this house by at least five years.

He was assigned to a guy named Frank Russo, "aka Frankaline," who showed Carmine around that night. They went over the layout of the firehouse: The first floor, where all the equipment was located; the second floor, where the administrative offices and officers' quarters were; and the third floor, where the bunks and TV room were located.

Then he had to show Frank that he could slide the pole. He already knew how to do this, but 1 Company was a three-story firehouse, which meant sliding from the third floor to the second floor, changing poles, and then sliding from the second floor to the apparatus floor. You had to be quick and in control or you would mess up the flow of men trying to respond. Frank showed him a different way to wrap his legs around the pole that allowed much more control. Carmine adopted this new method as his own.

He also learned about donating to the "coffee clutch." You contributed to this fund whether you drank coffee or not.

"They assigned me to the back step of Engine 1," Carmine recalls. He was the hydrant man that first night. He would stand in the middle on the back step of the engine and be the first to jump off at the hydrant and wrap the feedline around it. There were several false alarms that evening. "We really didn't do any fire fighting that night." But he had finally heard the sound of the bells hitting, slid the pole and ridden on the fire engine as a professional.

Just before midnight he turned in. Even though he was the junior man, he had a room of his own, a lucky beginning. "I was so excited, it was hard to go to sleep." He lay on his bunk staring at the ceiling, fully clothed. He wasn't sure how fast he could get dressed and didn't want to risk missing the call.

Not far away in the center of the city stood the old town hall and in its clock tower was a bell that rang on the hour. The firehouse had no air conditioning and the windows were wide open. At midnight, Carmine heard the bell from the clock tower. *Was it the firehouse bell?* He went into the hallway to see if anyone was getting up. No one was moving. *Not the right bell.* "The bell did hit, around 1 o'clock in the morning," he remembers, and he finally saw how it all worked and witnessed nineteen guys hitting three sets of poles.

"There are so many things you take for granted. You think you know what you're doing, but you don't even know how the bells really sound. You learn how to operate the watch desk and read the ticker tape to write out the addresses." You even have to learn how to lay out your gear.

Carmine had achieved a dream very early in his life. "There weren't that many people who were as gung-ho as I was," he says. The reality of the job was better than what he had dreamed of. The next morning he put the top down on his GTO and went home. He couldn't wait to come back and do it all over again...and again.

Chicago

Even gung-ho firefighters take vacations, and January 1971 found Carmine in Aruba.

One day in the hotel lobby, he spotted a man with a portfolio on which there was a Maltese cross. Carmine asked if he was a firefighter. Yes, he was, from Chicago. After about ten minutes of conversation, Carmine realized that he wasn't just any firefighter from Chicago. He was the chief of the Chicago Fire Department.

His name was Curtis W. Volkamer, and as Carmine discovered, he was a celebrated fire chief and a national and international speaker on fire science and technology. "Here I am, a rookie firefighter talking to a major figure in the fire suppression field," Carmine recalls. "At no time during our conversation did the chief ever act superior or act like he didn't have time to talk to the new kid." Instead, for about an hour, he discussed fire fighting procedures, asked the rookie how his department operated, and gave him encouragement that he remembered throughout his career.

At the end of the visit, Chief Volkamer said, "If you're ever in the Chicago area, give my office a call and we'll take good care of you." Feeling like he had just won the lottery, Carmine started planning his trip immediately. He wanted to see how things were done in the big city.

The next day he saw Chief Volkamer by the pool. After a few minutes of small talk, Carmine asked if he and a friend could take him up on his offer.

"Immediately the chief gave a positive response and took a piece of paper from his note pad and wrote down the name of his aide, with a phone number and address."

Volkamer left that afternoon, and Carmine spent the next two days dreaming of a trip to Chicago.

Back in Stamford, Carmine wrote to Volkamer. A response arrived, dated February 9, 1971. The chief himself had answered with a detailed letter about the proposed trip. "He even took the time to explain that his response was over a two-day period because he had responded to a five-alarm fire with one special alarm. His time at the fire scene was seven hours, yet this man took the time to write and make the rookie feel important."

Carmine and two of his firefighter friends, Pete Canzano and John Donch, made the trip. "We flew into O'Hare and waiting for us was a Fire Department car and driver. Our first step was to meet the chief at his office, and the VIP treatment lasted for four days." The three Stamford firefighters saw it all: the dispatch center, fireboats, the training academy, Snorkel Squad #1, the helicopter, and the famous "Big John" water cannon designed by the Chicago Fire Department. They were also invited to participate in the activities of Local 2 of the International Association of Firefighters. The visitors were assigned to the department's photo unit while they were in Chicago, which meant they went to many interesting fires. John Donch was an amateur cameraman, and says Carmine, "The photos and movies he took made everyone back home envious."

As a rookie, Carmine was assigned to #1 Mack. The Mack was a 1958 pumper that assisted with manpower and rolled in on most box alarms. It also handled the single engine calls in the center of the city. While he was in the Windy City, Carmine saw that the Chicago Fire Department engines had split hose beds that allowed double feed lines to be laid. Stamford at that time only laid a single line. "I remember telling my Captain, Eugene Callahan, that Chicago drops two lines and asked if we could try it. In a matter of weeks, Captain Callahan had plywood delivered and painted red; soon #1 Mack was doing the same thing the Chicago boys were doing – dropping a double feed line."

CARMINE STARTED PLANNING HIS TRIP IMMEDIATELY. HE WANTED TO SEE HOW THINGS WERE DONE IN THE BIG CITY.

PHONE BOOTH

CARMINE NEVER MADE PRANK PHONE CALLS as a child. But he made a few as an adult. So did most of the men at the fire station.

Fire Headquarters, where Carmine was assigned as a rookie, was on Main Street in downtown Stamford. Just outside the kitchen, mounted on the wall, was a classic rotary telephone. Surrounding it was a halo of graffiti: telephone numbers for pizza delivery, wives or girlfriends, and second jobs the men had on their days off.

During his first week on the job at Headquarters, Carmine noticed one particular group of guys running to use the phone just outside the kitchen. It didn't take long to figure out what they were up to.

About twenty-five feet away from Fire Headquarters, across the alley on the same side of Main Street, stood a bus stop. And at the bus stop was a glass-enclosed phone booth.

The men were making calls to the phone booth less than twenty-five feet away. From where the firehouse phone was you couldn't see the phone booth on the street. So the other men would act as lookouts. "Everyone would line up and watch out the windows. If you looked like a sucker, they would call you. If you were sitting at the bus stop, they would call the phone and let it ring and ring and ring until you got up and answered the phone."

JUST OUTSIDE THE KITCHEN, MOUNTED ON THE WALL, WAS A CLASSIC ROTARY TELEPHONE. SURROUNDING IT WAS A HALO OF GRAFFITI.

One day, remembers Bobby LaBlanc, there was a man sitting at the bus stop. The guys at the station dialed, the phone rang and rang, and finally the fellow in the booth picked it up. Bobby told him that he was at the phone booth earlier and threw something away and thinks he lost his watch. He asks the man to look through the garbage can. Good Samaritan that he is, the man at the phone booth digs through the garbage. Bobby tells him it was nice gold watch, and he really wants it back. The man digs more but has no luck. Bobby and the others at the station have a good laugh, of course, because there never was a watch.

Another classic prank was for one of the men to call the phone booth and pretend to be calling from the phone company. He would tell whoever answered that the lines needed to be cleaned out and ask the person to hold the phone out of the booth while they blew the lines. Most of the time they did it.

The neighborhood south of Main Street was showing some of the typical signs of decline; there were many bars and prostitution was readily available. "Girls were always walking Main Street," he said. As soon as someone spotted a "local girl" waiting by the phone they would run in and call her. They would joke with the girls, who knew exactly where the calls were coming from.

"Yeah, I remember dialing the phone," Carmine says. "I remember talking to a woman we knew as Emma." What he may have talked about is conveniently forgotten.

How did the firefighters know the phone number? With a grin Carmine says, "It was posted outside the kitchen."

Mynah Bird

Things get very urgent when you crawl into a burning building and hear a voice. Carmine had been on the job about a year when his engine and truck company responded to an apartment fire on Hope Street. It was a cold winter night, and snow covered the ground. "We were first due and I went in with a firefighter named Walt Finch. Walt had the nozzle and I was backing him up."

They went in the front door, into a vestibule. The fire was in a first floor apartment on the right of the entry. No one knew if there were people inside. "There was smoke showing when we arrived on the scene. We crawled in and Walt immediately found a woman on the floor. Together we took her out. She was still conscious." Instead of putting her out in the cold, they handed her off to the next team who set her in the hall so she would be sheltered from the cold.

They continued to work their way through the fire. "While we were gaining access, we could hear this sound that we thought was a person moaning. It was a kinda high pitched sound. It sounded like a human being. We knew we had someone in there we had to get out." Carmine and Walt signaled to the men behind them that they had another person to find. The information was relayed outside, and another ambulance was dispatched.

They searched furiously, everywhere: no one on the floor, no one on the bed or under it, no one anywhere.

The fire was in one bedroom but the moaning was coming from the other bedroom. The visibility was down to nothing. They searched furiously, everywhere: no one on the floor, no one on the bed or under it, no one anywhere. "Then the sound stopped. You're thinking there is this person dying close by and you can't find them."

As the smoke cleared they saw the source of the moaning. "There was a mynah bird in a cage about five feet off the floor. There was the bird laying on its side." It must have died from smoke inhalation while the men searched. Carmine was relieved that a human life had not been lost, but he still felt bad the bird had died. "The sound was so real," he said.

At right:
Carmine holds an original photo by Tom Ryan. The photo shows the dead bird in the cage on the front lawn after the fire has been knocked down.

MIKE CONTE

AFTER HIS FIRST WEEK ON THE JOB, and with a few fires under his belt, most of the guys had sized Carmine up. For his part, Carmine had watched and listened to each of them, forming his own opinions of them.

Some guys would be gung-ho, intricately weaving their engine and truck company duties into a smooth running operation. One or two, and they were easy to spot, would gladly volunteer to go back to the rig to retrieve the bolt cutter or an extra Halligan tool.

But from those early days, one guy stands out in Carmine's memories. "After a few weeks, Mike Conte came over to me while I was doing equipment checks and said, 'How ya' doing kid? Need any help?' Those seven words immediately made me feel like I was a part of their team."

It made quite an impression on Carmine: A senior guy was taking time out to make the rookie feel wanted, and he was going out of his way to offer him tips about how to improve on the job. Mike would frequently ask Carmine fire questions. "If I didn't give the correct answer, he would rephrase the question until I gave the answer that he wanted to hear. I thought the best part of the question and answer sessions was this guy taking the initiative to share some of his knowledge about the job with me."

It was after one of Mike's quizzes that Carmine was suckered into a Mike Conte joke. Conte would set you up with one sentence, or he would simply say "Did you hear the one about…" Throughout the department, almost everyone experienced Mike's spontaneous repertoire of jokes. Telling him you'd heard that one didn't stop him. He would simply tell you another, retrieving it instantly from some mental database of jokes.

If Mike did not snag you on the apparatus floor, he definitely would find you in the kitchen. One of Mike's firehouse assignments was running the "Coffee Clutch." Neatly tucked away in his wallet was a list of names indicating who had paid their dues for the month. The man assigned to the 6 a.m. watch desk duty also had the coffee making detail. "I remember Mike telling me 'if you make the coffee in the morning, include a sprinkle of salt. It takes out the bitterness.'"

There was a pool table and a Ping-Pong table in the basement of the station. Every time Carmine went downstairs to play, Mike would show up and say, "Kid, why ya' doing that? You'll never become chief unless you hit the books." Carmine remembers his response: "Mike, if you could remember the books like you remember the jokes, you would be chief of the world."

When they had to shovel snow off the ramp in front of the bay doors, Mike was the first one dressed. When they had to pack hose, Mike took the spot next to the running board, so he would have a captive audience. When anyone needed a break while on the watch desk, Mike offered his assistance.

When Carmine first had trouble tying knots, Mike told him how to tie a bowline. "Watch me. The rabbit comes up the hole, goes around the pole and back down the hole."

When Mike's son, Tony, was appointed to the job, he was a very proud man.

"I am sure there are many 'Mikes' in numerous professions across our country," Carmine says. "What made Mike Conte stand out then was his sincere willingness to help, that smirk on his face, and his medley of jokes."

In 1994 Mike retired after thirty-two years. Two years later a simple slip on wet leaves in his driveway left his body broken. He is now a quadriplegic. "Fortunately his mind is just as sharp as when we were on the job," Carmine says. Mike can still bring tears of laughter and sadness to Carmine's eyes. His jokes are still the same.

A guy had a friend that no matter what you said to him, he would come back with "It could be worse."

The guy says, "Did you hear about your next door neighbor?"

"No, what happened?"

"He came home from work and found his wife in bed with another man, so he shot both of them."

"It could be worse," the friend said.

"What do you mean, it could be worse?"

He said, "It could have happened yesterday when I was there."

"All rookie firefighters should be as fortunate as I was to have a Mike Conte looking out for them," Carmine says.

IT MADE QUITE AN IMPRESSION ON CARMINE: A SENIOR GUY WAS TAKING TIME OUT TO MAKE THE ROOKIE FEEL WANTED.

EVERYTHING ABOUT THE ALARM ROOM WAS OLD,
EVEN THIRTY-SOME YEARS AGO WHEN CARMINE WORKED THERE.

The Alarm Room

LIKE ALL PERSONNEL assigned to fire headquarters, Carmine had to learn the operation of the alarm room.

Everything about the alarm room was old, even thirty-some years ago when Carmine worked there. It was at the rear of the third floor of fire headquarters, a brick, stone, and concrete structure built in 1915. The equipment was old. The telephone was a black rotary model with a receiver that weighed about three pounds. Years of cigar and cigarette smoke had stained the walls and ceiling. The FCC licenses and typewritten instructions were faded in their metal frames. The green painted putty was falling out of the leaded glass windows. The small American flags taped to the tops of the old dark filing cabinets were faded. Even the smells, the products of decades and decades of use, were old.

"You entered the alarm room through a dark paneled wood door from the dimly lit third floor lobby," Carmine remembers. "Over the years the varnish covering the stain had cracked, and small lines like spider webs could be seen on the surface of the door when the lobby light shone on it just right. Every Friday the windows were washed and the brass was polished. The shiny brass doorknob on the entrance door has probably been polished more than a thousand times."

In the center of the alarm room, on a platform about eight inches off the floor, sat two antiquated dark gray switchboards. Each console was a duplicate of the other, so either operator could answer calls.

There were two operators, on eight-hour shifts, present at all times. On a rotating basis, firefighters would cover lunch, dinner, sick leave, and vacation time.

All dispatchers had to be Stamford firemen and they had to pass a test. Injured firemen were often assigned to dispatch to complete the last few years of service to the city; Local 786 took pride in taking care of its own.

Behind the dispatcher was the ticker tape where street boxes would punch four rounds of two-, three-, or four-digit numbers indicating which alarm box was sending a signal. The bell rang in cadence with the ticker tape punch. One dispatcher would count the punches. The other dispatcher would look up the number in the street files to know what apparatus to dispatch.

On the back wall, large double hung windows looked out over part of the city's decaying wood frame apartments and businesses. Many would eventually be damaged by fire or demolished by the wrecking ball allowing urban renewal the opportunity to create a new footprint for the city. On more than one occasion, after observing smoke or fire, dispatchers would transmit the alarm before an alarm from a pulled box or a phone call would reach the center.

When Carmine was assigned to the alarm room, Stamford did not have 911 service. In emergencies people dialed the police or fire departments just as they did any other telephone number. If they dialed 0 to report an emergency to the operator, their call would have to be transferred to the appropriate service. So most people kept the police and fire department numbers on or by their telephones.

Red lights on the console indicated calls on the emergency numbers; those calls were answered as quickly as possible. If one line was in service, it would roll over to the next, and the next, and the next. Today's modern dispatch centers are computerized, with back-up systems to make sure that emergencies are handled efficiently.

In Fire Headquarters, designated house lights were equipped with timers. Each time a bell would hit, the lights came on automatically. In cases when the dispatcher spotted a job while looking out the back window or took a phone call confirming a fire, they would sometimes hit the house lights. Knowing an alarm from a box was coming in, the crew could hit the poles earlier.In the alarm room of the 1970s, wit and knowledge of the city and the job took the place of some of today's computer systems. Firefighters were out the doors quicker then, Carmine says, especially if the dispatcher hit the house lights first.

Carmine was nervous the first few times he worked the alarm room. "The red light would light up like big red eyeball and the console would ring until you plugged into it," he says.

One afternoon the phones started ringing. The other guy on duty was a regular dispatcher and knew the job. He was forcing Carmine to take calls to train him. Carmine would say, "You get it." And the other guy would say, "No, you get it."

About five calls came in, and they all reported the same thing – a downed power line that was arcing. But every caller gave a different street and address. Carmine was confused. The other dispatcher said, "Just get 3 Engine rolling over there." So Carmine did. And then Box 217 came in.

"I didn't know that part of the city at all," Carmine says today. As it turned out, all the addresses were from The Village, a low-income housing project with a checkerboard of narrow alleys. It was near 3 Company, and with in a few years, Carmine would know it by heart.

At right:
Original running cards used to look up box alarms.

CHRISTMAS

MOST FIREFIGHTERS END UP WORKING one or more of the major holidays during the year. (In Stamford both Christmas Eve and Christmas Day are considered holidays.) In Carmine's first year on the job, his group was scheduled to work days on Christmas.

A normal day was ten hours, from 8 a.m. to 6 p.m., but, Carmine says, "As long as the lieutenant or captain was informed of your plans, it was not too important as to what time you arrived or left, as long as your relief was in to cover your position. This flexibility could work in your favor on a holiday like Christmas if you needed to come in a few minutes late because the children opened their presents."

Of course, Carmine's entire group wanted the day off, or at least to come in late. "It really didn't matter if you had children or not, you just wanted to have the day off." It didn't matter to Carmine at all: He was indifferent to working on holidays. It was another chance to catch a job.

Under a minimum manpower clause in the city's contract with Local 786, each firehouse could have a certain number of men off providing the number of men on duty did not fall below the minimum stated in the contract. The men would sign their names on the calendar in the captain's office a year ahead of time; then the allotted number of men could get the time off by the order in which they signed. "Inevitably, someone would always try to squeeze their name above the top name and attempt to beat the system," Carmine said. "At roll call Captain Eugene Callahan told us he had decided the best way to achieve our goal of getting time off for this holiday was to put slips of paper in the hat and draw." Drawing a "yes" meant you got the day off; a "no" meant you had to work.

The men with seniority who had already written their names on the calendar did not like the idea of drawing for time off. "But a few weeks before Christmas the lieutenant and captain summoned all twenty of us to the apparatus floor and the drawing took place. Three of the guys, Henry, Freddie and McNamara, volunteered to hold the hat but the lieutenant knew that they were up to no good."

Lieutenant O'Connor, who knew his men, ordered them to "open up both of your hands and let me see them." The men revealed slips of paper with "yes" on them. After some ridicule and good-natured ribbing, the captain said he would hold the hat and the lieutenant would pull the papers out.

"In the fire service, when all things are equal, seniority prevails, and this was one of those times. The senior man was handed his paper first and I would be the last to receive mine." The odds were dwindling quickly for Carmine. By the time it got down to the last two picks everyone knew there was one piece of paper in it with a "yes" and one with a "no."

"Already the group was making comments about doing it again – and we weren't even done doing it the first time. Naturally the 'yes' people at this point protested. The guy before me was handed a 'no.' That meant I had indeed accomplished the task of getting Christmas Day off my very first year on the job," Carmine says.

"My achievement lasted about two seconds."

He immediately felt a huge rough hand on his shoulder. "A deep voice coming from behind me clearly stated 'Carmine, you are not getting Christmas off.' As I turned around, I saw brother 'Bear' Silio standing there with a confident smile on his face." Bear had been assigned to the Truck Company, but he had been recently promoted to driving the deputy chief. On his days off he was a lobsterman on Long Island Sound. Standing about six feet, he had salt and pepper hair, a tanned face, and a solid physique. He took no bull from anyone.

Brother Bear explained to Carmine how he would enjoy Christmas at the firehouse. "Making the quick decision to allow the lobsterman to have my 'yes' piece of paper proved to be not so bad after all," Carmine says. He got time-and-a-half for working on Christmas. A local hotel prepared a complete turkey dinner for the entire house, and a restaurant sent over pies.

"We had a few runs but no fires. As the evening shift arrived there were still leftovers in the refrigerator," Carmine says. "We wished our relief a Merry Christmas and looked forward to seeing what Santa had brought us."

INEVITABLY, SOMEONE WOULD ALWAYS TRY TO SQUEEZE THEIR NAME ABOVE THE TOP NAME AND ATTEMPT TO BEAT THE SYSTEM.

SODA BOTTLES

SOMETIMES GROWN MEN DO STUPID THINGS.

Fighting fires is stressful and exhausting. Sometimes you just have to let go. In between runs there's a lot to do, but just like any other job, it is easy to find time to goof off.

Training for fires and medical emergencies takes many repetitious hours; there is no room for error when you arrive on the scene. A day can go by very quickly when you are becoming familiar with structures in your response area, doing public education, studying, checking your equipment or taking time to sit down and have a prize winning meal by one of the guys. But there are times when acting stupid just happens.

On the corner of West Main Street and Fairfield Avenue there was a bus stop with a green wooden bench, and as Carmine remembers, "Sometimes we would go sit out there and just goof off even though we weren't really supposed to be sitting at the bus stop."

It was the middle of the day. 3 Engine had just come back from a run. It was an ordinary sort of run, an automobile accident. The men had to remove the victim from the car. Because it was a hot summer day the man wore very little clothing, only a pair of cut-off shorts and no underwear. The victim happened to be very well endowed. And there lies the problem.

Back at the station, Carmine recalls, "We were all feeling rather deficient. If I'm not mistaken, it was the captain's idea to put a bottle in his pants and go sit at the bus stop. He was sitting there with the soda bottle in his pants with one of the other guys when I walked out of the station. Immediately I had to get a soda bottle, figuring if they can do it, then it's okay for me to do."

So there they sat in their blue work uniforms, hoping someone would notice them and acknowledge their greatness. No one gave them a second look.

"We were three jerks sitting at the bus stop, with our legs spread open showing off our well endowed bottles," Carmine says. For about ten minutes they sat there, admiring themselves. Then the bells went off. "We had to run back to the firehouse with the bottles in our pants." Three grown men – firefighters, heroes – went racing back to the firehouse, holding their groins and laughing hysterically. Looking back on it, Carmine admits it was not one of their – or his – shining moments. "It took a lot of guts, or maybe stupidity," he says.

Fortunately the bus never came. And none of them tripped on the run back to the firehouse.

"Captain, He Bought Eggs"

When his transfer papers came, Carmine discovered he was assigned to 3 Company, Group 4. As of the next shift he would report to "The Hill," the West Side, where he grew up. "That is where I definitely wanted to go. 3 Engine was turning into one of the city's busiest engines because we were in the midst of urban redevelopment. This was the best place to be for action. I was excited about arriving there. They were getting more and more working fires." He wanted to get dirty.

Carmine knew most of the crew because he had rolled in with them on other calls. Captain McAuliffe was a cool-headed twenty-five year veteran fireman; nothing bothered him, Carmine says. But like most captains, he had his "own little quirks about how things get done." So he showed Carmine around and gave him a brief orientation.

On his first day at 3 Company, there was only one call before lunch – a false alarm, Box 217 at the corner of Victory and Pressprich in the Village, a low income housing project. Then it was time for the junior man – Carmine – to go to the grocery store and get the sausage, peppers and French bread for the sandwiches they ate almost every day.

As Carmine was getting ready to leave, the captain said, "By the way, don't forget a half-dozen eggs." Carmine made a mental note and off he went to the store, hurrying because to miss a call would be a tragedy.

The moment Carmine returned to the second floor kitchen, one of the firemen looked in the bags. "Where's the eggs?" he asked. Carmine was confused. *The eggs are right on top. Can't Jimmy see them? Did I buy the wrong kind of eggs? My first day, my first trip to the store – have I messed up already?* The fireman yelled down the hallway, "Cap, can you come here for a minute?" The captain, who was in his office doing paperwork from the earlier call, came strolling down the hallway.

"Cap, he bought eggs."

The captain said, "He bought eggs?"

"He bought eggs." The fireman held up the evidence.

The captain exclaimed "He bought eggs!!!"

Carmine was bewildered and desperately trying to figure out what he had done wrong.

"The captain put his hand on my shoulder and said, 'Son, when I tell you to buy a half-dozen eggs, the name of the eggs is Budweiser.'"

MY FIRST DAY, MY FIRST TRIP TO THE STORE – HAVE I MESSED UP ALREADY?

The Couch

Style and décor were not big issues up on The Hill. The couch in the dayroom on the second floor of 3 Company was proof of that. It was a basic couch from the 1950s or 1960s, covered in black vinyl – cheap black vinyl. "It had so many rips in it that you could see the white lining and foam in the cushions," Carmine recalls. "It was perfect for us. There wasn't anything new in our station."

Unfortunately, the couch also was home to a variety of bugs, but that didn't stop most of the men from sitting on it. Carmine, a little more selective, avoided the couch for the most part.

They had the couch sprayed several times, but the bugs kept coming back. So did the bug man. "The bug man had a big old fat cigar. The cigar stunk more than the junk he sprayed around." The bug man had perfect timing, too. He would usually show up for his monthly spraying right before or during lunch.

One day the men decided that the couch had to go. Their intentions were honorable: They planned to carry the couch down the stairs and dispose of it properly like good city employees. But that idea was quickly scrapped. "There was no impact by doing it that way," Carmine says. So they pushed the couch out the second floor window.

"Bobby LaBlanc, the captain, was one of the ringleaders of this thing. I remember standing on West Main Street on the sidewalk with Bobby next to me." Carmine had just bought an 8mm. movie camera and wanted to record the entire event. The dark green sash window was lifted and the couch was precariously balanced on the sill.

The men waited for Carmine's signal. The camera rolled and the couch fell to its death. It took one bounce and lay there, intact. They all cheered and claimed a victory: Man over Furniture.

"We couldn't leave it there," Carmine says. So they took it to the curb and called the city garage and told them that a piece of furniture had fallen off a truck in front of the fire house and needed to be picked up.

The evidence of their lie – the movie film – still exists, kept in a secret location. "I never liked that couch," Carmine admits today.

Bobby LaBlanc didn't care much for the couch himself. He remembers that day, and a few other peculiarities of the station. "3 Station was a filthy, filthy place," he says. "I couldn't stand it. That's why we threw the couch out. I painted the whole place myself."

One day, Bobby asked Carmine to clean the stove. "He took all the parts and went outside. I went to my office, I'm typing away, all of the sudden I hear BOOM. I look out, and I see all black smoke. I thought, *Oh, Christ, the car wash exploded out back*. No, it was Carmine. He filled this thing up with gasoline, put all the stove parts in it and threw a match in it to clean the grease. Geez, it was smoking."

At right:
The original 8mm film footage of the couch being tossed out the window.

ONE DAY THE MEN DECIDED THAT
THE COUCH HAD TO GO.

THE DOG

FIREFIGHTERS TAKE PRIDE in saving property and lives, and they understand that a pet is part of the family. But once in a great while, a thoughtless action by one firefighter can give them all a black eye, especially when it makes them appear insensitive to someone's loss.

One evening, 3 Station received a call for a three-story, six-family wood frame apartment on Greenwich Avenue. "When we pulled up the whole top floor was going pretty good," Captain Bobby LaBlanc remembers.

While advancing their handlines in the crew came across a big beautiful dog, a cross between a Labrador and a Shepherd. "He looked like he was sleeping," Carmine says. But he wasn't sleeping. He was dead, probably from smoke inhalation. "After the fire was knocked down, I moved him out of the way into a corner of the kitchen." Carmine didn't want plaster and wood falling on the dog as the firefighters walked through to overhaul the apartment.

When the woman who lived in the apartment came home to find her apartment destroyed, she was clearly upset. She immediately began asking about her dog. The deputy chief on duty tried to comfort her. He called to the men upstairs and asked if they had a dog up there. They said they did. The chief said to bring it down.

The problem was that instead of bringing the dog down from the third floor, someone threw him off the third floor porch.

Carmine was rolling up hose on the ground, his back to the house. "I heard the dog come down, I heard the thud," he says. Bobby LaBlanc, who was standing near by at the time, says "The dog landed right at the woman's feet." The woman became hysterical, and the deputy chief took her around to the front of the house, away from her pet.

"I was astonished that anyone in their right mind would throw a dog off the third floor porch," Carmine says. "I went upstairs and asked repeatedly, 'Who threw the dog off?'" Finally someone owned up to the deed, only to be chewed out by an angry Carmine.

To add insult to injury, during the overhaul, the debris from the third floor was shoveled off the porch and onto the dog below. "The only thing sticking out was the tail," LaBlanc says.

What happened after that is lost in memory, except for one thing: the crews of 2 Company and 3 Company let their thoughtless colleague know in no uncertain terms that he had been unnecessarily unkind to someone they were pledged to help.

ONCE IN A GREAT WHILE, A THOUGHTLESS ACTION BY ONE FIREFIGHTER CAN GIVE THEM ALL A BLACK EYE.

At right:
Particles of smoke from an apartment fire attach themselves to spider webs.

The New 3 Truck

In the late 1970s, the City of Stamford started a campaign to replace aging fire equipment. For 3 Company, this meant a new 100-foot aerial ladder truck to replace an old 85-foot ladder truck. The new truck, equipped with a variety of tools to help ventilate structures, was state-of-the-art for its time. It was a large investment for the city.

The firehouse rumor was that no one had measured the doors to make sure the new truck would fit inside. "You would like to believe that the higher echelon of city government would think things out before they buy a piece of equipment that's probably close to a half a million dollars," Carmine says.

As it turned out, the rumors were right. The doors were either not tall enough or wide enough, or both. "3 Company was a beautiful two-bay firehouse built in 1910. The doors were old green wooden doors with thick leaded glass panels from floor to ceiling. Now all of this had to be removed so that they can put in one giant overhead door."

While the engineers and architects were redesigning the front of 3 Company, it was also determined that the floor was not strong enough to support the new piece of equipment or 3 Engine which was still in use. "We were told there was a possibility of the floor collapsing."

The station had a full basement, where the emergency generator was and where the firefighters hung their gear when not on duty. The engineers decided to install screw jacks in the basement to hold up the apparatus floor. About every eight feet or so there was a floor-to-ceiling jack.

Replacing the two old doors with one overhead door was a complicated job. To accommodate the new door, the engineers, said, the pillar between the two old doors had to go. But that was a structural element, and to maintain the structural integrity of the door opening they proposed to span the entrance with steel beams.

For all these years they had two pieces of equipment parked inside. Now all of the sudden they had to leave the equipment outside in the driveway. 3 Engine had a big blue tarp on it to protect it from the elements. "It didn't work out too bad except when we had heavy rains." Meanwhile, the new 3 Truck, which had arrived before any of the work had started, had to be kept at another firehouse until the construction was complete. "This doesn't take place overnight." It took months.

"Parking was at a premium to begin with," Carmine says, and it soon became a bigger problem. As it was, the firefighters had to play parking roulette at shift change. When a new group arrived to work, the current group would move their cars to street parking so the next shift could use the small strip of parking that ran along the station.

The alterations changed the entire look and feel of the station. Where there had been two green wooden doors there was now one overhead door. And the new bricks didn't have the same texture or color as the seventy-year-old bricks. Thanks to the jacks supporting the apparatus floor, Carmine says, "the basement looked like a prison. From back to front, from wall to wall, they were there until the building was demolished."

THE FIREHOUSE RUMOR WAS THAT NO ONE HAD MEASURED THE DOORS
TO MAKE SURE THE NEW TRUCK WOULD FIT INSIDE.

THEN, CARMINE THINKS, HE THREW HIS HELMET OUT THE OPEN WINDOW.

The Helmet

It was about 2 a.m. one summer morning in 1975 and there was a working fire at a near-by three-story wood-frame multiple family dwelling. The firefighters knew they had a job. "You could see it when we pulled out of the station. You could see a little glow in the sky."

They were at the fire in less than a minute. "There was quite a bit of fire showing out of the second and third floor windows. The residents on the street were yelling that there were people inside the building." The people on the street were scared and hysterical, pulling at the firefighters' coats as they tried to get inside. Carmine was on one of the nozzles. "We advanced the line into the building up to the second floor," he says, while at the same time 3 Truck was putting its aerial ladder up to the roof. Carmine had a back-up man right behind him. Another team went to the third floor with their handline. All of them were thinking there were still people in the building.

They crawled into one room and then into another. "We were searching apartments, looking on and under beds, on couches and in closets. Visibility is almost zero, just about everything is by feel." At some point he got separated from the man behind him, something that normally would not happen.

He had not finished searching the second floor when his air supply alarm went off. "The bell was ringing on my Scott Air Pac. I was with the nozzle. That's your lifeline. You have about three to four minutes left depending on how heavy you are breathing." The alarm going off means you need to leave the building, Carmine knew, but he also knew there might be a human life at stake.

"Sometimes you take risks that are not in your best interest, but you make split second decisions when you are in situations." Carmine kept going, crawling into one room and then another, searching.

"I'm sucking in the air like crazy while I'm crawling through the rooms." Then the air was gone. He knew he came in the front door and could follow the line out. But he also saw what he thought was an open window.

He took in that first deep breath of hot noxious smoke and felt nauseous. "You can't hold your breath, you have to breathe. Then you have to pull your mask off. Your body is screaming for air. But there is no air. At this point you're scared. You consider yourself one of America's bravest, but you're frightened for your life."

He was in the front bedroom. *I've got a problem here*, he thought, *I've gotta somehow get out of here. I know I'm not gonna make it out.* Then, Carmine thinks, he threw his helmet out the open window, a signal to the firefighters on the ground that someone is in trouble. He needed help –immediately.

In a room full of smoke, with your oxygen gone, you rapidly begin to lose your senses. "That's where the story gets foggy. I thought I followed the hose line back with my nose down to the ground and tried to get down the stairs." But the driver of 3 Engine, Donald Smith, remembers a different story. He says he told Carmine to come out the window. "He tells me he broke my fall when I came out the window. I don't remember."

Falling out a second floor window would have been a desperate measure. Falling out with an air pac on your back adds another element of danger. But it was a desperate situation. He does, however, have a clear memory of waking up. "The only thing I remember is waking up in a puddle between the curb and the sidewalk. I remember saying to myself, 'They put me in a puddle.' " Standing over him were some firemen. "I was fine." He sat on the back step of the engine and took in some oxygen. One of the firemen took him to the hospital in the deputy chief's car to get checked out; Carmine refused to go by ambulance. What was done at the hospital is something else Carmine can't recall. He just remembers walking out during the shift change at about 8 a.m.

Carmine hates not remembering how he got out, but he believes Smith's version of the night. "Donald's story makes more sense. I was already out of air, why would I crawl back through the smoke to go down the stairs? Your mind plays funny tricks on you when you don't have enough oxygen."

For the record, there was no one in the building.

Box 217

EVERY CITY HAS A BAD NEIGHBORHOOD. Stamford's was a low-income housing project known as Southfield Village. Southfield Village was on the west side of Stamford, about two miles from 3 Station, and in the center of the project, at the corner of Victory and Pressprich Streets, was the red fire alarm box 217. The three 8-story mid-rise buildings and several 2-story buildings that made up Southfield Village were built in the 1950s — no parks or grass, just cement and dirt. They were poured concrete and block, and, says Carmine, "they acted like ovens when a fire occurred inside." Open-air hallways on the exterior allowed the fire to remain contained in the apartment of origin.

Many of the residents of Southfield Village did not have telephones. Box 217 was their only way to report a fire or medical emergency. They knew they would get immediate response from the fire department. "A minimum of once every shift you would go to Box 217, usually for a false alarm. But it wasn't uncommon to go there three or four times in a twenty-four-hour period," he says. Often it was because garbage had been set on fire in the hallways or someone was stuck in an elevator, but most times the alarm was pulled by kids with nothing to do.

It was so common to see the fire department arrive in Southfield Village that the engines never drew crowds the way they do in middle class neighborhoods.

The stairwells always smelled of urine and the elevators rarely worked. The firefighters would pull their handlines up the stairs, stepping over the garbage. For fires on upper floors they would advance their lines on the aerial ladder up to the balcony. The buildings had standpipe connections, vertical five-inch pipes in the building stairwells that the engine could pump water through, but they couldn't risk using them. "We never hooked up to the standpipe, you never know what could be in the there. They could be filled up with soda bottles, beer bottles, stones, dead rats."

The firefighters knew the layout of the apartments by heart. They were small with very little furniture in them. "There were either no sheets on a mattress sitting on a frame or the floor, or a fitted sheet so filthy that I don't know what color it might have been when it was put on." And then of course there were the cockroaches. "I can remember being on the nozzle and crawling into one apartment on the upper floor of 85 Pressprich and seeing these brown things on the floors and walls. They were exiting while we were crawling in." In the aftermath of a fire, they would remove the kitchen cabinets to make sure the fire had not extended into the walls. "There would be hundreds and hundreds of cockroaches that survived. Smoke doesn't bother those guys." The men would check their gear and each other for bugs when they came back outside. "It was not uncommon to go back to the firehouse and shake out your clothes."

IT WAS SO COMMON TO SEE THE FIRE DEPARTMENT ARRIVE IN SOUTHFIELD VILLAGE THAT THE ENGINES NEVER DREW CROWDS THE WAY THEY DO IN MIDDLE CLASS NEIGHBORHOODS.

At one point the city spent a considerable amount of money for emergency lights and exit signs and they flushed out all the standpipes in an effort to bring the complex up to fire code. "That lasted about a week," he says with a touch of sarcasm. "The Village kept 3 Engine busy but it became redundant."

"When we would go there in the wee hours of the morning, we would see children playing baseball or basketball in the streets." The kids used sticks for bats and seemed oblivious to the fact that there was broken glass all over the streets. "People would set their apartments on fire intentionally knowing that if they were burned out they would get better housing." Even though Carmine loved fighting fires and getting dirty, responding to Box 217 every day was frustrating. Like he wanted, somehow, to make their lives better but he didn't know how.

Southfield Village was demolished in 1998, and a new affordable low-income city housing project is rising in its place.

Pictured above and at right:
Views of the Southfield Village Housing Project.

THE EYEBALL

3 ENGINE RESPONDED TO MANY CALLS that did not involve fires. Once they were sent to find an eyeball.

Merrell Avenue was another one of Stamford's low-income housing projects, a complex of several mid-rise apartment buildings. "We would always go to Merrell Avenue not so much for fires but for stuck elevators." Each engine had a tool box filled with door keys for almost every elevator manufacturer, and says Carmine, "We became very efficient at opening elevators."

"The call came in this day for 3 Engine to assist in looking for an eyeball." That's what Captain Bobby Lablanc told them. A child, about 12, was playing in the shaft on top of the elevator and it moved. His head was caught between the elevator box and the interior wall of the shaft. "We were told his face was crushed in on one side. You couldn't tell if his eyeball was still in his head or not." 3 Engine didn't have to rescue the boy. He was already at the hospital when the engine rolled in. Someone in the emergency room requested that the Fire Department search for the eyeball.

"The bottoms of these elevator shafts are concrete pits, partly filled with the dirtiest, filthiest brown water and garbage. There's years of debris that has fallen down between the cracks. It stinks." The crew disabled the elevator. "We took a roof ladder off the engine and put it down into the elevator pit. I went down the ladder, which wasn't very far, about 5 feet." The other guys were leaning over the side of the shaft watching Carmine, who had probably volunteered to go down.

The water is only about a foot or two deep, but it is disgusting.

"How we gonna find an eyeball in here?" Carmine said. "And then the largest cockroach in the history of Stamford crawled across the floating debris." He hates cockroaches, and this was a big one. "If that eyeball is in here it's in his stomach," somebody said.

Carmine spent no more than three minutes looking around for the eyeball. "I'll tell ya' the truth I didn't know if eyeballs floated or they sank." As it turned out, the eyeball was still in the child's head. It had been pushed inside.

The boy lost his sight in the one eye but survived, and Carmine saw him several times years later.

Captain LaBlanc had to write a report about this call, as he did about any call. As a result, Carmine says, "There is an eyeball report floating around in the Stamford Fire Department archives somewhere."

At right:
Elevator shaft at the Merrell Avenue Housing Project.

THESE ELEVATOR SHAFTS ARE CONCRETE PITS...THERE'S YEARS OF
DEBRIS THAT HAS FALLEN DOWN BETWEEN THE CRACKS.

Winding the Bells

There are different daily assignments in the firehouse. The drivers take care of the apparatus floor; the junior man cleans the toilets and so on. There is one assignment called orderly, and the man that draws it fills in the gaps doing odd jobs, one of which is to wind the bells. Each bell had a key and wound up like a clock. Just about the time of roll call, the orderly would check the bells.

"On The Hill, we had a bell up on the second floor on the wall outside the bunk room and one on the first floor by the watch desk. And when they rang it was loud. You could hear them outside and they woke you up at night."

If a fire alarm box is pulled then the box number would hit on the bells at the fire house, for four rounds. Each time the bells hit, it would wind them down. "At that time, it didn't matter where you were in the city, if someone pulled a box, it would ring in every single firehouse." So on a busy shift, the bells had to be wound often.

Then came a night with a lot of runs. 3 Engine alone had gone to two working fires. "We were exhausted when we came back." Carmine thinks it was probably about 3 o'clock in the morning. They just wanted to go lie down.

"This is where the story gets pretty good. We're all in the bunk room. It's funny how you hear things you wanna hear on the radio. There's a radio in the captain's office. And we hear '3 Engine where you located?' I think I heard it twice. What we were hearing was the deputy chief who had responded to the box on West Main and Spruce Street," only about 100 yards away.

They all got up and were slightly confused. "The box was pulled and we never heard it." The orderly checked the bells and sure enough they needed to be wound. "We've missed the call, we're first due!" somebody exclaimed.

The box at West Main and Spruce was famous for false alarms. "West Main and Spruce was usually pulled by the garbage men, although we couldn't prove it," Carmine says. It didn't happen every morning, but it happened often enough. The garbage men would pass by the station deliberately banging the cans around and then at West Main and Spruce they would pull the alarm.

The captain picked up his walkie-talkie. He needed to answer the chief. Carmine thinks he told the deputy that 3 Engine was having mechanical difficulty. The deputy chief confirmed the false alarm, sent the other engines home and came up to The Hill. The captain had to confess the truth. The chief knew the men had been working all night, he had been right there with them. "Nobody intentionally forgot to wind the bells."

After that, whenever the men came back, someone always checked the bells, whether they were the orderly for the day or not. "We were very fortunate that it was a false alarm. It never happened again."

EACH BELL HAD A KEY AND WOUND UP LIKE A CLOCK.

MENTORING GREGORY CLOUD

ONE DAY IN MAY 1975, A KID SHOWED UP at the firehouse. He had seen the firemen jump off the back step of 3 Engine and stop traffic so the engine could back into the station, and he came over to watch. Carmine was standing in the street doing his job.

"I looked at him. He looked at me. It started with a simple 'Hi.'" says Gregory Cloud.

Gregory lived around the corner from 3 Company, and as Carmine had when he was a kid, he walked by the station many times.

Carmine remembers their meeting, too. "He was about as tall as the wheel on the fire engine – he wasn't even that tall when we first met him."

Carmine immediately liked Gregory, who was about ten and knew he wanted to be a fireman. That first day, Carmine took Gregory inside. They sat on the old bench that had the names of firemen carved into it and talked for about an hour. He also gave Gregory some fire magazines, which he promptly read and brought back the next day. Carmine then showed him all the equipment and let him try on one of the Scott Air Pacs. It about tipped him over.

Whenever Group 4 was on duty, Gregory would stop by and visit. "I was in heaven," Gregory says.

"He grew up with us," Carmine says. "We trusted him to the point that we would go out on calls and leave him in the firehouse." He became part of the firehouse family. Gregory would push the button to open the doors and let them back in. The neighborhood children would laugh at

him for hanging out at the station. Gregory didn't care. He was right where he wanted to be. "Gregory was a sharp kid. He became part of us," Carmine said.

From the time he was about two years old, Gregory wanted to be a firefighter, just as Carmine had. "I believe it was in my blood," Gregory says today. Carmine and Gregory bonded instantly. "I was here when he was here," Gregory says. "I knew Carmine's schedule." Gregory wanted to know about the jobs they had gone to. Together they would listen to the scanner and hear about fires in New York City. Gregory memorized the codes and learned to decipher the emergencies.

One day Carmine took Gregory to the South Bronx to see Engine 82, the busiest engine in the United States at that time. They spent several hours watching the engine come and go and talking with the men of 82 Engine and 31 Truck. When he was sixteen, Gregory wanted to join the Air Force because they would make him a firefighter. Carmine encouraged Gregory to be patient, stay in school, and at eighteen take the Stamford test. He took Carmine's advice, and he has been working at 3 Company for more than nineteen years. "Needless to say, I am tremendously proud of him because he eventually became a firefighter," Carmine said. Gregory is

At right:
Gregory Cloud holds a photo of himself
(at approximately age 12) on 3 Truck while
standing in front of 3 Engine which he now drives.
Photo of young Gregory by Carmine Speranza.

He grew up with us…We trusted him to the point that we would go out on calls and leave him in the firehouse.

now the driver of 3 Engine, the engine Carmine was assigned to the day they met.

They never fought a fire together, but as Chief Fire Marshal, Carmine would see Gregory after a fire had been knocked down. Carmine would ask him, "What did you see when you went in there?"

Mentoring is a rewarding job. Most of the time you may not even realize you are doing it. If you are proud of what you do, then it is easy to share your knowledge, especially with children. Carmine never saw Gregory as a burden; he loved sharing his passion with a young man who seemed just like him. "He learned to trust and respect the firefighters and in turn they learned to trust and respect him," Carmine says. Gregory says the same thing, "He respected me, I respected him."

MENTORING IS A REWARDING JOB. MOST OF THE TIME YOU MAY NOT EVEN REALIZE YOU ARE DOING IT.

At left:
Gregory and Carmine lean against the last remaining wall of the old 3 Company.

BOBBY LaBLANC

BOBBY LaBLANC FIGURES IN MANY of Carmine's stories, and in fact, he was the ringleader in the escapade of the soda bottles and the flight of the couch. He joined the Stamford Fire Department in 1959, ten years ahead of Carmine, and retired as deputy chief in 1989, five years before Carmine.

Like Carmine, he is a font of memories and stories. Many of them involve the housing project known as The Village.

"There was a kid in the village who knew how to short out the whole electrical system," he remembers. "We couldn't figure out how he put those elevators out of commission all the time." But LaBlanc and the firemen finally found out. "He used to go up to the eighth floor with a roll of tinsel from a Christmas tree. He'd make a ball of it, and from the eighth floor he could make an arc over the three high power lines and short them out. He was a genius."

Fire department work wasn't always about fires. Bobby remembers responding to one alarm in The Village that certainly wasn't. "There was a guy standing there at the door," LaBlanc says. "I said, 'Is this your apartment?'"

"Yeah, it's my apartment."

"Where's the key?"

"I don't have a key. You gotta get the door open."

"I said to Carm, 'Get a bar and force this door open.'"

They wrenched the door open. "There's this guy standing there with the other guy's wife," Bobby says. "Staring right at us. I was the first one in the door. The guy's behind me and they started in on each other. I said, 'There's no fire. This is a police matter, let's get out of here.' I went back and told the chief, 'I am not forcing any more doors without police protection.' And that's when that started. What if the other guy had a gun?"

Elevator problems were a fact of daily life in the housing projects. And sometimes the toolbox filled with elevator keys the engine carried wouldn't do the job. "In one particular building they had a bad elevator and with the equipment we had, you needed a broom handle. If an elevator got stuck on the eleventh floor, you had to go up on the adjoining car and get alongside of it and look through the little slit. We had a broom stick, and you pop the broomstick in there and it would pop the adjoining door."

One morning they got a call about the elevator. "There's a guy stuck in there. It was about 4:30 or 5:00 a.m. when we got there. I yelled up to the guy, 'What floor ya on?'

He said, "'I'm on 13, but there ain't no 13, so you mash 14.'

"So we get up alongside of him, and as soon as Carm sticks the broom in, the car moved. It was like that for an hour, back and forth; we could not get along side of him. The guy was screaming, 'You better get me the hell outta here.'

"'What's the matter?' I said.

"'This son of a bitch is coming home from work at 6 o'clock.'

"'What are you doing in there? Oh never mind I got it.' Now I'm nervous for the guy, I don't want him to get caught.

64

"'Are you mashing 14?' he says.

"'Yeah, I mashed everything.'

"I can't get this car to stop, the main door was open. I tell him, 'I'll get you out one way or another.' Like I'm rooting for him.

"He screams, 'It's not like you have to get me out, you better get me out.'

"I said to Carmine, 'I can't stand it anymore.' I started to shake the mechanism and it went off the track. And the bottom part of the door popped about three feet. He crawled out and he ran like a snake down the stairs. Just in time, too. He no sooner got out of the driveway, than the other guy came home. Left her in the elevator."

Calls to The Village were frequent. "I had been to the village as a lieutenant about three hundred times," Bobby remembers. "But my first call as a captain came on a Thanksgiving Day. It was a dryer in the basement. I took off my helmet, put my radio down, went to look under the dryer. When I turned around, everything was gone; oh, yeah, all gone. *Geez*, I thought, *I can't go back and tell them somebody stole my stuff*. So I got a hold of the oldest kid there. I said, 'You gotta do me a favor. Look, we came over here to give you a hand. I am not your enemy. I'm gonna lose my job.' I pleaded with him. He brought my radio back. Had to be some older kids, I figured."

THAT STUFF IS GONNA BLOW UP

CHEMICAL PLANTS CAN POSE SERIOUS PROBLEMS for firefighters, particularly when the firefighters don't know what chemicals are on the premises.

The first alarm for the Polycast Chemical Company fire, Bobby LaBlanc recalls, came at about 5 a.m.

"We were first due here. When we pulled up, I said to Carm, 'It's quiet here. There's no sign of smoke but there's something wrong.'" All the air conditioning units in the windows were hanging out, ready to fall on the street.

"The watchman told me they had a little problem, but it's okay, they can take care of it. Everybody said, 'Let's go back, there's nothing visible.'" So they went back to the station.

The Advocate [the local newspaper] called Bobby in his office. "The reporter asked, 'What's up with Polycast?'"

"'Well,' I said, 'I don't know.' Then 'bing,' the bell hits again."

It was Polycast again, Bobby says, "only this time, the place is on fire."

When they arrived this time, they found that the sprinklers had been activated. "They took in a couple of inch and a half lines," Bobby says. "There was a refrigerator I could see down the hall; the door had blown off of it.

"I wondered, *What the hell is going on in here*? I got hold of the night watchman. He says, 'They got a chemical in here called C-110, something like that. Something to do with making plastic.'"

Bobby went into the office and called the Chemtrex twenty-four hour hotline for chemical problems. Someone picked up right away.

"I said, 'This is Captain LaBlanc, Stamford Fire Department. We've had a little problem here with a chemical called C-110.

"The guy says to me, 'C-110? Where are you now?'"

"I said, 'I'm in the office.'"

"'Of that building?'"

"'Yeah.'"

"'Well, get the hell out of there, that stuff is gonna blow up.'"

"So I threw the phone down and ran out the side of the building. I came running down the street yelling 'Get the hell out of there everybody.'"

At six o'clock the next day, Bobby says, "We had to go back there. These little bottles were in there ready to go. I guess the bomb squad took them away.

At right:
The watch desk at Engine 2, Stamford's oldest firehouse.

ABOUT A MONTH AFTER THE TEST, TENSIONS START TO RISE.
THE GUYS ALL KNOW WHAT'S COMING.

PROMOTIONS

THE STAMFORD FIRE DEPARTMENT gives promotional tests about every two years. The weeks before the test are stressful enough, but the four to six weeks of waiting for results can be downright agonizing.

When he took the lieutenant's test for the first time, Carmine was working up on The Hill at 3 Company. Captain Bobby LaBlanc gave the candidates all the material he knew they needed to know, and whenever Carmine saw another guy cracking a book, he would do the same. "I was studying quite a bit, but not enough," he says. "I took the test and didn't feel super-confident about it but didn't feel very badly about it either."

Everybody tries to figure out which questions they got right and which they got wrong. Carmine kept track of all the questions he could remember and the ones he heard others talking about in case he saw them on another test. On the bottom shelf of a bookcase in his study is the twenty-year-old spiral notebook in which he kept his notes, complete with marginal notes and yellow highlighting. To this day he remembers the questions he got right and wrong.

About a month after the test, tensions start to rise. The guys all know what's coming. "Rumors start flying around: the test results are gonna be in the mail tomorrow, they've arrived at City Hall." Carmine, like most of the others, could not wait for the mail to bring the results to his house. Early in the morning he would drive to the Springdale Post Office, hoping to pick up a white legal-size envelope containing a congratulatory letter.

"I drove the car over," he remembers. "I didn't take anyone with me; I was really uptight. I sat in the car first because I was really nervous. I didn't go right in. I finally had the guts to walk in." In the pile of mail he was handed was the white envelope with his name on it. He went back to the car, holding his envelope in one hand and the rest of the mail in the other. Sitting in the car, he was nervous and scared. "I said a prayer and opened it." His heart was beating rapidly, and he could hardly focus on the paper, but a third of the way down the page, he saw what he dreaded. There was an X in a box by a line saying "You have failed to achieve a passing grade." Says Carmine, "The part I remember seeing was 'you have failed to achieve,'" he says. "It didn't matter what else it said."

He was devastated. "I flunked." He still seems amazed and hurt by this defeat. There he was, a cocky, gung-ho firefighter, shot down. How would he face his family? How would he face the men he worked with, even though he knew some of them had flunked too? The anxiety he felt that day, he says, was the same as the day he received his draft notice.

Angry with himself, Carmine knew he had two years to study and redeem this misstep. "I needed to fail the first one," he says. "It gave me two more years, and many more fires under my belt. It gave

Top left: captain's hat.
Bottom left: firefighter's hat.
Bottom right: lieutenant's hat.

me more practical experience that you can't get from a book." The "you failed" letter went up on a wall at his house as a reminder of what he needed to do.

Two years later he found himself sitting in the same parking space at the Springdale Post Office. Once again, he had a white legal size envelope in his hand. He debated whether to open it there or take it home. Once again, he offered up a short prayer, and then ripped it open. This time he saw the words he had waited two years to read: "You have attained a passing grade, your ranking is number 8." He looked up at the ceiling of his car and offered up another short prayer: "Thank you, Lord, thank you, thank you."

He never failed another promotion test.

TWO YEARS LATER HE FOUND HIMSELF SITTING IN THE SAME PARKING SPACE AT THE SPRINGDALE POST OFFICE. ONCE AGAIN, HE HAD A WHITE LEGAL SIZE ENVELOPE IN HIS HAND.

SHIFTING GEARS

CARMINE WAS ACTING CAPTAIN AT 5 COMPANY for a few days. He had been there before. He knew the men, and he had total confidence in them. But one day two factors came together to make it a day to forget – or to remember: The regular engine driver was off, and Engine 5 was out of service and a reserve unit was in the bay.

"The unit turns out to be an antique, a 1950 Mack fire engine with an open cab and a big silver bell," Carmine recalls. Reserve Engine 5 had rolled on two short calls that day. "He (who shall remain nameless) wasn't the best driver in the world, but he got us there."

Then came the third call for the day. This time they had trouble getting out of the station. "I knew we were in trouble when we got in the apparatus to respond and we backed up three times. This was a stick-shift engine. He couldn't get it in gear to go forward. We kept going backwards."

The engine was first due at the alarm, but Carmine knew that would never happen. To get there they had to drive up Fifth Street, a steep incline. Engine 5 started up the hill, but any momentum it had was lost when the driver tried to shift gears. They would have to stop and start all over again in first gear.

"It was very embarrassing to the point where I stopped blowing the siren. I didn't want anyone to even know we were going to a fire."

Then came the truly embarrassing moment. A kid on a ten-speed bike pulled alongside the engine as it struggled up the hill at about ten miles an hour and asked Carmine, "Hey, where's the fire?" He was mortified. The kid on the bike was pedaling faster than the engine. He had slowed down to ask about the fire and then sped up the hill and reached the fire before 5 Engine could get there. They arrived third due and were not needed. The crew saw the kid on the bike at the scene, and one of them yelled at Carmine, "Hey, lieutenant, isn't that the kid who passed us on the bicycle?" Not wanting to risk more ridicule, Carmine asked another man to drive them back to the station.

The original driver showed no remorse for his inability to handle the antique apparatus. Carmine was silent, but the three other men assigned to the engine had plenty to say to the driver. "He had to take the heat from the guys on the back step," Carmine says. That was punishment enough.

At right:
View from the driver's seat of the 1950 Mack truck they drove that day.

72

THE UNIT TURNED OUT TO BE AN ANTIQUE, A 1950 MACK FIRE ENGINE WITH AN OPEN CAB AND A BIG SILVER BELL.

Sunday Morning

It was a peaceful Sunday morning. The men of 5 Company had just finished breakfast, and the men had begun to attend to their details for the day. Carmine, who was back at 5 Company for a few weeks as acting captain, had started to study for the captain's exam. A loud rumble rolled through the firehouse. *Are they testing the generator?* Carmine wondered to himself. *But it's the wrong day to test the generator.* Back to silence. After a couple of minutes he heard himself paged over the PA system. "Cap, can you come down to the apparatus floor?" He was, he recalls, immediately suspicious. "Just the way they said it made me think something is not right."

Down the stairs and through the vestibule he walked, slowly, giving the men time to get their story together. He couldn't see the problem right away. But when he came around the corner, he says, "There's the engine sticking through the door. And the door is down."

5 Company was a new building at the time. The doors were solid panels with a row of glass windows at eye level. "The front of this engine was sticking out about three feet. The door was wrapped around the front of the engine. Obviously the sound I heard earlier was the engine going through the door."

He couldn't believe it. Here he was, not wanting anything to tarnish his assignment as acting captain, and now he would have to explain how a fire engine had gone through a closed door – and stand by his men at the same time. He knew it was an accident, but he also knew it did not look good no matter how it happened. All he could think was, *I'm responsible for all this.*

He started asking the men what happened, and they kept saying, "Cap, you don't want to know." The problem was, he needed to know. "I had to write an incident report that was factual but kept my men out of trouble."

Carmine took 5 Engine out of service and called the deputy chief at Fire Dispatch by telephone, avoiding the radio for the sake of discretion. As the 5 Company crew stood outside along busy Washington Boulevard waiting for the chief, they noticed that traffic was starting to slow down and stare at the engine protruding through the door. So before the chief arrived they quietly moved the engine into another bay, and Carmine started his paperwork about the morning's events.

The most likely explanation was that the engine, a stick shift, was left in gear with the brake off. Someone accidentally hit the ignition button while reaching in to do the daily check of the lights, which made the engine jump forward. There were four firefighters working on the floor at the time. "There are at least two men who know the truth." But Carmine isn't one of them. "To this day," he says, a big smile on his face, "I do not know the exact story."

The damage to the engine was slight – only some scratched paint – but the large hole in the door had to be boarded up. The four foot by eight foot sheets of plywood patching the door made it obvious what had happened, and it took about a month to repair the panels. By lunch that day, the men were joking about it. After all, it was just an accident; they didn't do it on purpose.

At right:
Original log book with entry by
Acting Captain Carmine Speranza.

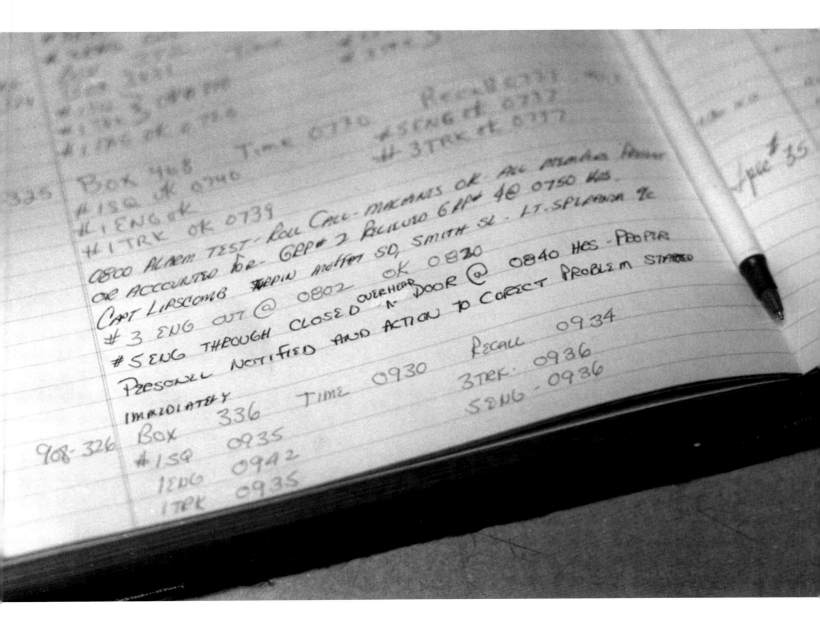

ALL HE COULD THINK WAS, I'M RESPONSIBLE FOR ALL THIS.

EMBERS WERE DROPPING EVERYWHERE
AND COULD CATCH ANYTHING COMBUSTIBLE ON FIRE.

THE FODI FURNITURE FIRE

SUNDAY MAY 4, 1978, started like any hot summer Sunday in Stamford – slowly. Carmine was acting captain at 4 Company, located in an upscale beach neighborhood that overlooks Long Island Sound. It was not one of the busier firehouses. There was not much action there, not like 3 Company, up on The Hill.

Listening to the radio, Carmine knew several other engines were out on brush fires, and he hoped 4 Company would be called on soon. "I heard an engine from headquarters being dispatched to a dumpster fire. The odds were getting pretty good that my engine was gonna be dispatched next."

Carmine knew before the bells hit that they would be called. He had heard the captain from Engine 1 call dispatch over the radio and say "Transmit the box, we have a working fire."

"Looking out the front door, I couldn't see anything in the air yet," Carmine remembers. But he told the men, "Hey, we're going out." The five-man crew was dressed before the bells went off.

The dumpster was adjacent to the loading dock of the Fodi Furniture Store, which occupied the entire first floor of a 4-story brick apartment building. The flames spread quickly and caught the wooden back porches of the structure on fire.

4 Company was across town from the scene. As they were on their way, they could see large

At left:
View of the three houses on Relay Place. The center house still shows fire damage that has never been repaired. The other two houses have been renovated. The Fodi complex was located behind the houses.

volumes of smoke in the sky. "The captain of Engine 1 was now reporting that fire was showing out of two buildings and starting to move onto the next exposure," Carmine says. "The deputy chief was also transmitting an additional alarm prior to his arrival." By the time Carmine and his men arrived the flames had engulfed all the buildings.

"My assignment was to go down a dead end side street called Relay Place. We had three two- and three-story wood frame homes that had smoke or fire showing from the attics. Once we pulled into the street, we were committed. We couldn't turn around. There was parking on both sides of the street and room for only one piece of equipment." There was about two to three feet on either side between the engine and the parked cars. Once the engine was there, no one could pass it.

"There were civilians running all around the place. Some were trying to move their cars, but we had them blocked in." Embers were dropping everywhere and could catch anything combustible on fire. The houses were very close together. It would take enormous team effort to save these homes.

4 Engine, also known as a tele-squirt, is different from the other engines. It is equipped with a 55-foot boom with a master stream nozzle attached at the end. Using this boom, they started to pour a curtain of water on the houses to keep them cool. "The paint on the side of the buildings was already turning brown, the radiated and convected heat was getting to them. I told my crew to take a two-and-a-half-inch line into the attic where fire is showing."

At this time they were the only piece of equipment working on this part of the fire. Carmine knew they had to quickly knock down the fire and get to the next house. "We were responsible for the houses on this street."

He ran down the block to check on other houses and when he came back he couldn't believe what he saw his crew doing. "I see them pulling a one-and-a-half-inch line inside." He yells, "No, I don't want an inch and a half, I want a two-and-a-half-inch up in there. And one of the firefighters said to me, 'Cap, we don't pull two-and-a-half-inch lines into a building.'"

"Take the two-and-a-half-inch line up there, he says, and just darken the fire down because we have to get into another building." Carmine was stunned by their actions.

Usually a one-and-a-half-inch line was the largest hose they pulled into a fire building. Under normal circumstances, this would have been quite sufficient. "This was not a normal circumstance. I wanted a lot of water fast. The wind was blowing the fire my way." He remembers looking out the attic window of one of the houses and realizing the situation was out of control. "The whole block at this time was roaring. It was a wall of fire." The entire Fodi Furniture complex was involved.

His crew completed their job with the assistance of another engine that had pulled in behind them. "We lost the attics and parts of the roofs." But the residents at least had homes to come back to even though there was considerable water damage. As the evening wore on, the crew of Engine 4 was assigned to assist the other firefighters. Eight engines and four trucks worked well after dark that night.

"Dumpsters don't catch on fire by themselves," Carmine says. "In my opinion, the human element assisted in the start of this fire. I am sure they never imagined it would take out a whole city block." But that's just what it did. "This single engine call turned out to be one of Stamford's largest fires."

THE WHOLE BLOCK AT THIS TIME WAS ROARING. IT WAS A WALL OF FIRE.

THE CROW

AFTER MAKING LIEUTENANT, Carmine was transferred into a new group and station. The deputy chief there was a seasoned fireman who was known around the department as "The Crow." He could run a fire scene with ease, but he was occasionally forgetful about some parts of everyday life.

One evening he came to work at six and forgot to shut his car off. Every one of the twenty-one men assigned to the house soon knew about it, but, amazingly, they all forgot to tell him. At six in the morning, a voice announced over the public address system, "It's still running." At 8 a.m. "The Crow" got into his car and drove home.

But it was the everyday use of the English language that was The Crow's biggest challenge. "Often we would come back from a run and one of the guys would say, 'He did it again.'" Carmine says. "And then he would tell a story in which a phrase was used that had very little meaning to anyone but The Crow."

Simple terms were mangled in strange ways. The Holiday Inn Crown Plaza Hotel in Stamford became "The Holiday Johnson." Radial tires became "radical tires." Thermal underwear became "terminal underwear." Domestic help became "doministic help." The magnolia tree across from the fire station became a "mangolia tree."

Some of his most memorable lapses in language came in the course of fighting fires, and since they were often made over the radio, they spread instantly. He was known for ordering a feed line by saying, "Lay me a two-incher," and a double feed line (two parallel lines) by ordering "Lay two paralyzed lines." When he asked dispatch to replay their phone tapes so he could get some more information about a fire scene, what went out over the radio was a request to "Play back your playbacker." But his greatest radio command came at the Fodi Furniture fire, when he realized that more than a city block was threatened and more equipment was needed on the scene. His order was as simple and direct as it was mangled and memorable: "Send me everything you've got." You can hear that one echoing throughout the Stamford fire department still.

It wasn't just in the heat of fighting fires that The Crow's language got garbled. He once asked another fireman if he was to be his driver that night by asking, "You riding me tonight?" Once, after an early morning run, he told his colleagues, "I don't know whether to get up or stay up." Recommending that a situation be taken as it comes, or played by ear, he told the crew, "Let's play it ear by ear."

The business, training, and social side of fire fighting brought out some of his best verbal miscues. After the union signed a new contract including provisions for retroactive pay, he was heard to comment on "radioactive pay." After a class on child birth, in which firemen were taught how to cut an umbilical cord, The Crow was ready to "cut the biblical cord." And at one Fire Department social event, he ordered a carafe of wine, which came out as a "giraffe of wine."

Everyday life also gave him plenty of opportunity to mangle the language. His son, who was on the waiting list to be hired by the Police Department, was described as "an alternator" on the Police

Department hiring list. The son was married to an Oriental woman. In The Crow's fractured English, he had "married one of those ornamental girls." Speaking of a rental deal that included the utilities, he remarked that "All utensils are included in the rent." And to provide for his future, he invested, not in the stock market, but in "the stocking market."

There would always be at least one guy with a notebook keeping track of these flights of anguished language, which were then critiqued around the kitchen tables during mealtimes.

"Each time we thought one couldn't be topped, a new one would surface," Carmine says. "The guys with seniority, Jukie, Hurl, George, and Richie, would immediately use the quote in a sentence. Standing around the coffeepot or on the apparatus floor, doing your house chores, or picking up hose after a fire, you could be sure to hear a "crowism."

It was as if, to borrow one of The Crow's phrases, what he heard "came in one ear and out the next."

He was a character, says Carmine. "From his evening ice cream runs to the countless hours of laughter he brought our group, there can only be one Crow and we will miss him."

HE COULD RUN A FIRE SCENE WITH EASE, BUT HE WAS OCCASIONALLY FORGETFUL ABOUT SOME PARTS OF EVERYDAY LIFE.

81

The Last Day

Twenty-four years after he started what he calls "the greatest job in the world," Carmine knew it was coming to an end. "You know you are going to retire months ahead of time," Carmine says. "You've chosen the date in your mind."

For thirteen months in 1992 and 1993, Carmine served as acting chief while Stamford searched the nation for a new fire chief. Although he was one of three finalists in that search, he wasn't selected. The day after he knew he was not going to be chief, he told the contractors to start work on his new house in Florida.

He spent the next year and a half as chief fire marshal, assisting Chief Ron Grainer. At the end of that time, retirement became a reality.

As the final day approached, people wanted to take him out to lunch and dinner, friends wanted to say goodbye, wanted to say they would miss him. Stories got told over and over, and it seemed as if the day would never come.

But come it did. On the morning Carmine went to work for the last time, there was cake and coffee waiting for him. *This is my day,* he thought. *Tomorrow I am going to be in a car driving to Florida.* The house was sold, the movers were on their way south. His wife was already in Florida. "I was sure I was making the right decision."

He made the rounds of all the offices and then drove to 3 Company and 2 Company to see some of his brother firefighters. "Your emotions move between excitement and sadness. Subconsciously, I knew I was going to miss the job."

Richie June came to say goodbye. "Chief," he said, "I am really sorry to see you go. But the sooner you go, the sooner we all get a chance to move up the ladder, and maybe I'll get my chance to be a lieutenant now." Richie, a knowledgeable, experienced, firefighter, is currently a lieutenant.

Carmine turned in his city car in the middle of the afternoon, and then he needed a ride home. Chief Grainer asked "Are you ready to go?" "Yeah, well, I guess so," he responded. They drove over to the Government Center so Carmine could see some people at the 911 Dispatch. From there, home (a rented apartment) was only a mile away. On the radio Whitney Houston sang "One Moment in Time." In the driveway, the Chief shook his hand and thanked him for his dedicated service. "He told me that it's a good thing I'm doing, retiring." Grainer had retired himself and come back to work so he knew what Carmine was feeling.

Before Carmine got out of the car Grainer handed him the radio microphone. Carmine wouldn't say anything, so Grainer called dispatch himself: "Stand by for a message from Chief Speranza," he said. He passed Carmine the radio. "I didn't know what I was going to say," he remembers. But with some emotion, he managed to thank his comrades and say he would miss them.

As they parted, Carmine and Grainer saluted each other. Carmine watched Grainer drive away. He stood there with his briefcase and a small box of items from his office. He turned and started up the stairs, but, he says, "I sat down on the first landing and started crying." Thinking, *Did I do the right thing? I just finished a career that no one could duplicate. No one could ever have a better job.*

He tried to sleep that night because he was driving to Florida the next day to begin a new phase of his life. At 4 a.m. he was wide awake; by 4:30 a.m. he was on I-95 South.

I am done. I am never coming back. I am retired.

Afterword

It is no secret that I always wanted to be a firefighter. I have said on more than one occasion that it is the greatest job in the world. In my opinion, it can not be topped by any other profession.

Every time the bell hits, you never know what situation you're rolling into. You are required to make decisions rapidly – decisions that can shape the outcome of somebody's life or your own.

Just because you're on an engine – whether the lights and sirens are on or off – the public responds to your presence. People look up to you, they respect your profession.

People call us because they need our expertise *immediately*. They can't wait hours for the services we provide. In most cases, we are not going to have them arrested. We are there to help and provide comfort. Saving a life is a wonderful feeling, but knowing you were able to contain a fire and save the family photos, diplomas, or that precious pet, is also a reason to be proud. The long hours of training always pay off.

Fire fighting is a job in which working together as a team makes the outcome even better than doing it by yourself. Some times you know more about your fire house family than you do about your own extended family. Private lives and work lives are intertwined. You know when a child is sick or someone is going through a divorce. Crew members share in the good times and the bad.

And when a son or daughter follows in the footsteps of a family firefighter, creating a legacy, the reward is great.

Fire fighting is a job in which working together as a team makes the outcome even better than doing it by yourself.

Wearing your class A uniform or your daily blue work uniform becomes part of your commitment to provide a service that very few are chosen to perform.

In twenty-four years of fighting fire, I saw a lot of changes. Since my retirement in 1993, I have seen still more. But they come slowly.

Fire fighting is entrenched in tradition. Once a piece of equipment has worked well, it takes extensive research to introduce something new. Every month new products are marketed in professional fire publications. Some look like great ideas but they are expensive, while others might not be practical for all departments.

The fire services have learned to design by disaster. It often takes a catastrophic fire with loss of life or significant monetary damage to spur new laws and fire codes.

In 1978, for example, four Stamford firefighters were severely burned in an explosion at a chemical plant. They were all very experienced in fire ground tactics, but before they entered the structure, an explosion trapped them in an alley, exposing them to a fireball. Their exposed clothing, made in part of polyester, melted to their

At right:
Carmine Speranza, 2001.

skin. Cleaning the burns – removing the melted clothing and other debris – before treating them was very painful.

Two of the firefighters had to retire because of their burns; the other two eventually returned to work.

At the time, polyester pants and shirts were standard issue for Stamford firefighters. New fire department regulations that require cotton work uniforms were quick in coming, but it took a disaster to bring that about.

Another improvement prompted by that chemical fire was a Connecticut law known as the "Right to Know" law, which requires businesses to report to the fire department all hazardous materials stored on the property.

When I first came on the job in 1969, the lead engine did not have self-contained breathing apparatus. The only breathing protection used was a charcoal-filtered mask, and in most cases it wasn't worn. In the minds of many firemen, it took a real man to enter a smoke filled building. And real men didn't wear masks. Back in those days, exiting the building with sooty faces and snot hanging from your nose was part of the job. Today's firefighters wear air packs even at motor vehicle fires, because cars today are loaded with plastics that produce poisonous smoke when they burn.

Today's firefighters are better trained, better equipped, and better protected, thanks to the sacrifices of their predecessors.

Today's firefighter is fully encapsulated – protected from head to foot. When I started, some of the seasoned men refused to give up their rubber coats, and they would never pull up their boots. But the traditional rubber coats and boots did not allow the body to ventilate itself enough. Gloves made of fire-resistant material replaced the orange rubber gloves, which were prone to melt when hot objects were handled.

I can remember being on medical calls where the only breathing device used on a patient was a resuscitator. CPR was not yet part of the department's procedures, and watching someone's cheeks flutter from a blocked airway was all too common. Today, firefighters are cross-trained in providing emergency medical care. They are now an extension of the hospital's emergency departments, trained to use defibrillators and to maintain airways through intubation. This was a natural evolution, as the fire department is always the first to respond. If they are going to rescue someone, they need to be able to treat that person, too. Today, many fire departments, including Stamford, identify themselves as fire and rescue services.

Thirty years ago the Halligan was the primary forcible entry tool. Using the Halligan and a flat head ax, firemen would break through storefront overhead rolling grates, locked doors, and motor vehicles involved in crashes. The Hurst Tool, or "Jaws of Life" that is seen so often on television news, was developed for professional auto racing, not the fire service, but today it is carried on most fire and rescue apparatus.

A five-inch diameter feed line was a dream, not standard for engines. The feed line, which was two-and-a-half inches, supplies water from the hydrant to the engine. The introduction of one-and-three-quarter-inch handlines with variable flow nozzles made the job more efficient. Previous choices were a one-and-a-half-inch or booster line. The booster line was totally inadequate for interior fire fighting because it did not deliver sufficient gallons of water per minute. I used booster lines to put out grass fires as a volunteer firefighter, and I knew it was not good enough then.

We rode standing on the back step of the engine, many times still trying to get our gear on as the engine pulled out the door. Today's firefighter rides in a jump seat with a roof overhead that protects against the elements and any thrown objects. (Unfortunately, in the 1970s, throwing bricks, bottles and stones at authority figures was common.)

Having your tank and mask mounted in your jump seat behind you has saved quite a bit of time upon arriving at the fire scene. In my day, the masks and tanks were packed in a suitcase in a side cabinet on the engine. Each time we got to a fire we had to unload and assemble the units for each man.

Remember that $60 device called a smoke detector? Just attach it to the ceiling and it would alert you if smoke was in your home. Twelve thousand people were dying in fires across the United States each year during that era.

Who would ever think firefighters would wear hearing protection while responding? Certainly we didn't when I was a firefighter. The louder the siren, the more people knew we were coming. Many older firefighters now have hearing problems because of the constant exposure to sirens and air horns.

A program that taught school children to "Stop, Drop, and Roll" has saved thousands of children and their families from death and severe injury. Developed by the National Fire Protection Association (NFPA), firefighters taught school teachers and the teachers taught the children. It was a standard curriculum so everyone would learn the same methods.

MUCH CHANGED FOR FIREFIGHTERS in the course of my twenty-four-year career. The hard work and physical sacrifices that many firefighters across America have put into the profession have not gone unnoticed. Today's firefighters are better trained, better equipped, and better protected, thanks to the sacrifices of their predecessors. And the people they serve – the public – are better protected, as well. The future can only be safer.

Those of us who fought fires in the 1970s and 1980s did not have some of today's equipment, or training. But we stayed busy. Like many cities, Stamford went through an identity crisis. Stamford worked very hard to bring corporate America into the center core of the city. But sad to say, urban renewal often led to the crime of arson. Building owners could make money from the insurance industry by having more than one fire in the same three- or four-story wood-frame railroad flat. The challenge for an owner who knew the property was on a site where a new high-rise or corporate headquarters was planned was to see how many fires could take place before the big one hits.

Fires would usually start in rubbish piled in the halls, allowing the smoke to travel up the vertical opening. If that did not scare the tenants out, fires would start in vacant apartments or the basement.

As I said, we kept busy in those days. It was not unusual to pull out of the engine house and see an orange glow or large column of grayish black smoke in the sky. One-and-a-half inch hand lines were the first line of attack, and pulling up your boots was a must to help keep your knees from being burned as you advanced your line in.

Your gear, hair, and clothes stunk of smoke when you returned to your station. Two-and-a-half-inch hose would be laid out on the apparatus floor drying from the working fire of the day before.

Morale was high. There were lots of fires. It was great to be a firefighter in the 1970s and 1980s.

It was okay to be the junior man. You would be in the hose bed packing hose, or standing in the middle on the back step ready to take the hydrant. You knew how to wrap a hydrant and watch as the feed lines flapped off down the street, listening to the distinct sound of each fifty-foot length hitting the pavement.

You couldn't wait until the pump operator broke the line and hooked it to his pump panel so you could open the hydrant that supplied the water that would knock down the fire. Then you could walk up to the engine and mask up and go in and get to work.

Not only did we fight fires, we also had to avoid the rocks, bottles, and trash cans thrown at us simply because we were part of the system.

You always felt out of place when you were issued new equipment to wear because yours would be so clean and that of the rest of the crew dirty and smoky. Fortunately, after only a few jobs your clothing would look just as dirty as the guy working alongside you.

The firefighter's slogan – "Firefighter, Americas Bravest" – could not have been more true in those days. Not only did we fight fires, we also had to avoid the rocks, bottles, and trash cans thrown at us simply because we were part of the system. During roll call my deputy chief once commented, "If we are attacked again and we don't have the police present, I'll give the order to chop the feed line and drive away."

I remember having a union bumper sticker that said "Firefighters fight fires, not people."

After retiring in July of 1993 my goal was to be associated with an agency that would keep me involved in the field of disasters. The American Red Cross fit that requirement.

My wife, who is a registered emergency department nurse, and I had the opportunity to travel to major conventions across the United States for almost two years. Our assignment was to recruit medical and emergency service personal to be part of teams that respond to disasters for approximately three-week assignments.

One of the most educational disasters I responded to as a Damage Assessment Specialist was the Los Angeles earthquake of 1994. From a firefighter's point of view, it was very interesting to see how buildings moved and what the effects would be for the incoming fire units.

Another area of involvement is a Disaster Medical Assistance Team, or DMAT. This unit is part of the Department of Health and is activated by the government when cities need assistance during a major disaster. Many states have these units; belonging to one is probably the closest you can get to being in the military without actually getting drafted again. A highlight for our team was to have members assigned to Fort Dix, New Jersey, for a three-week assignment to assist in processing the Kosovo Refugees in 1999.

I also participate in the Florida Governor's Hurricane Conference, a week-long event held each May, before the official start of the hurricane season. Working behind the scenes is great. This is the largest conference of this kind and it takes teamwork to pull it off. It is a wonderful opportunity to meet many of the emergency planners from the twenty-six states that attend.

Another very rewarding part of my retirement has been the opportunity to be a chaperone for a snow camp for severely burned children at the Adaptive Sports Center in Crested Butte, Colorado. Each winter, a group of children from Florida ages twelve to sixteen enjoy one week of non-stop fun involving skiing, snowboarding and more. The lessons learned from this experience are both humbling and gratifying. As one camper

simply put it last year, "I might look different on the outside but I'm the same as you on the inside."

That's my story. And those are my stories. I thank Beth Reynolds for making it possible for me to tell them, and for her photography, which adds so much to them. And I thank Clint Page, whose editing helped me tell them.

Retirement is a great thing, but I would give almost all of it away if I could have the opportunity to be back on the job again. The politics that go with a chief officer's job I could do without. In my opinion, your crew comes first. Just put me on a busy engine company, and I would come home with a smile on my face every day.

Carmine Speranza
September 2001